BUSINESS BASICS Series

Focuses on a variety of situations involved in business and provides opportunities to improve learners' communication skills in the workplace.

BUSINESS BASICS 1

CARROT HOUSE

Business Basics 1
© Carrot House

All rights reserved. No part of this publication may be reproduced, stored in a retrieval system, or transmitted in any form or by any means without the prior permission in writing of Carrot House

Printed: January 2023

Author: Carrot Language Lab

ISBN 978-89-6732-114-7

Printed and distributed in Korea
268-20 Itaewon-ro, Hannam-dong, Yongsan-gu, Seoul, Korea

Curriculum Map

CARROT

Course	Level 1	Level 2	Level 3	Level 4	Level 5	Level 6	Level 7	Text Book
General Conversation	Essential English : Begin Again							
	Pre Get Up to Speed 1~2							
		New Get Up to Speed+ 1~2						
			New Get Up to Speed+ 3~4					
				New Get Up to Speed+ 5~6				
						New Get Up to Speed+ 7~8		
	Daily Focused English 1							
		Daily Focused English 2						
Discussion			Active Discussion 1					
				Active Discussion 2				
					Dynamic Discussion			
			Chicken Soup Course					
				Dynamic Information & Digital Technology				
Business Conversation	Pre Business Basics 1							
		Pre Business Basics 2						
			Business Basics 1					
				Business Basics 2				
					Business Practice 1			
						Business Practice 2		
Global Biz Workshop				Effective Business Writing Skills (Workbook)				
				Effective Presentation Skills (Workbook)				
					Effective Negotiation Skills (Workbook)			
					Cross-Cultural Training 1~2 (Workbook)			
					Leadership Training Course (Workbook)			
Business Skills				Simple & Clear Technical Writing Skills				
				Effective Business Writing Skills				
				Effective Meeting Skills				
				Business Communication (Negotiation)				
				Effective Presentation Skills				
					Marketing 1			
						Marketing 2		
						Management		
On the Job English				Armed forces 1				
				Armed forces 2				
				Aviation 1				
				Aviation 2				
			English for Cabin Crew					
			English for Call Centers					
			English for Medical Professionals					
				English for Aviation Maintenance Technicians				

※ This Curriculum Map illustrates the entire line-up of textbooks at CARROT HOUSE.

CARROT HOUSE

Business Basics 1

Introduction

Carrot House Methodology

Andragogical Approach & Productive English

The teaching of children (pedagogy) and adult learning (andragogy) are distinctively different. Pedagogy is akin to training and encourages convergent thinking and rote learning. It is compulsory, centered on the teacher and the imparting of information with minimal control by the learner. Andragogy, by contrast, is about education as freedom. It encourages divergent thinking and active learning. It is voluntary, learner oriented and opens up vistas for continuing learning. Adults need to feel independent and in control of their learning. Therefore, Carrot House curriculum is based on andragogy and is designed to encourage learners' participation and engagement by providing more task-based activities and opportunities to frequently interact in the classroom.

People want to achieve communicative competence when they learn other languages. English education in EFL environments has been rather focused on the receptive skills of English—listening and reading—which simply increases learners' knowledge about a language, not the competence of using it. If people are well equipped with productive skills—speaking and writing—they will be competent in English communication.

This is why Carrot House curriculum is designed to enhance learners' productive skills throughout the course. This andragogical approach of the Carrot House Curriculum, which focuses on productive English, will enable learners to achieve communication skills necessary for global competence. Carrot House's teaching philosophy and curriculum combine to provide a "Language for Success" for all learners.

Communicative Language Learning (CLL)

This communicative interaction, the essential component of language acquisition, does not occur in a typical, non-meaningful, fun-oriented conversation with native speakers. It occurs in a negotiated interaction through which a well-trained teacher provides the comprehensible input that is appropriate to the learners. The learners, at the same time, actively utilize the opportunities given to them by the teachers.

To this end, the Communicative Language Learning (CLL) method is employed in the field of Foreign Language Acquisition. The CLL method provides activities that are geared toward using language pragmatically, authentically and functionally with the intention of achieving meaningful purposes.

Course Overview

I. Objectives

BUSINESS BASICS Series is designed to enhance learners' communication skills in the workplace by providing a wide range of situations involved in business. Each series is targeted at intermediate level learners. Through constant classroom interactions, learners can improve their productivity proficiency to achieve success in international transactional situations.

II. How to Use Business Basics 1

II-1 Lesson Composition

The book consists of 16 lessons (4 units) based on topics of great interest to everyone involved in business. The composition of each lesson is as below.

Learning Objectives

Set clear goals to acknowledge target learning of each lesson.
- Go over the learning objectives with learners to understand the learning focus.
- Review the objectives at the end of each lesson to reinforce each point.

Getting Started

Stimulate learners' thinking and put them at ease in an English speaking environment through situation-related questions and expression questions with visual aids.
- Open the class with discussions questions and encourage learners to brainstorm answers together.
- Use the visual aid to allow learners to practice expressing their ideas and opinions.
- Encourage learners to deliver short speeches as a warm up activity.

Good to Know: Common Mistakes

Provides learners with language practice on commonly made mistakes.
- Learners review and correct commonly made errors through activities.
- To be used flexibly.

Language Practice

Reinforce useful business expressions and patterns through substitution drills. Learners will practice how to use the essential expressions within their business lives.
- Have learners study the expression and learn how to apply it in various situations.
- Have learners review expression and key patterns by creating their own sentences.

Quote of the Day

Presents famous quotes for learners to reflect upon and express their own opinions.
- Learners can reflect on the quote and discuss their opinions through answering the discussion questions.
- To be used flexibly.

Business Basics 1

Situation & Dialogue
Understand the mission of each business character and role play to practice English speaking in business situations. Help learners improve their comprehension skills and utilize useful expressions.

- Have learners answer questions about the characters to check their understanding of the mission and business situation.
- Pair up class to practice the dialogue and compare with their own work.
- Give feedback on each learner's role play.
- Allow learners' to answer the discussion comprehension questions.

Case Scenarios
Reinforce learners' response skills in various business situations through case scenarios activities. This will enable learners to apply the thematic situations and the skills of global business communication.

- Pair up class to review each scenario.
- Have learners follow each stage to create dialogue and role play using the background information provided.
- Give feedback on each learner's role play.
- Each lesson has 2 case scenarios to review.

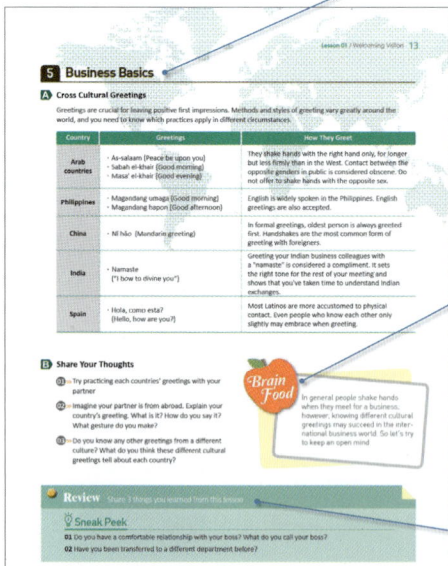

Business Basics
Expand learners' ability to develop essential business skills, such as making presentations, taking part in meetings, telephoning, and using English in social situations. Learners will learn business manners or etiquette through the medium of English.

- Have learners read the background information and complete the task as a pair or as group work.
- Encourage learners to 'share their thoughts' by sharing their personal experience, ideas and opinions in more depth.

Food for Thought
Provides learners' with additional information regarding the Business Basics theme.

- Allow learners time to read the information and open the class for discussion or opinions.
- To be used flexibly.

Review & Preview
Recall and review material learned each lesson as well as preview the following lesson through discussion topics.

- Go through review questions with learners to follow up on learning objectives mentioned at the start of the lesson.
- Discuss preview questions to lead up to the following lesson topic.

II-2 Case Studies

Each unit includes a Case Study. The Case Studies are based on realistic business situations and problems. They will encourage students to develop communication skills and problem solving skills by giving them opportunities to practice in realistic business situations.

Background Information
Have learners read and understand background information about the company and situation.

Task
Have learners complete an activity that encourages them to think about the problem in each case study and how the company or individual can address the problem.
- Pair up or form groups to talk about the problem.
- Ask learners to think about how the problem should be dealt with.

Presentation
Encourage learners to present their solutions as they would in real business situations.
- Allow individual or group work to present solutions, the logic behind the solutions, and their expected outcomes.

CONTENTS

Unit 1. Daily Office Routines

Lesson Title	Learning Objectives	Language Practice	Business Basics	Page
Lesson 01 **Welcoming Visitors**	- to be able to greet and guide visitors - to be able to introduce yourself, the company and your colleagues	· I'm in charge of... · Allow me to... · Could you direct me to...?	Different Cultural Greetings	10
Lesson 02 **Organizational Structure**	- to understand and discuss different organizational structures of companies - to discuss roles and responsibilities of different departments	· I suspect that... · I might as well... · Have you heard about...?	Flexibility in the Workplace- Hot Desking	14
Lesson 03 **Collaborating with Co-workers**	- to discuss various ways to get along positively with co-workers - to talk about different working relationships	· What do you think about...? · I can't stand... · Would you mind if...?	Great Business Partners	18
Lesson 04 **Dealing with Conflicts**	- to explore different ways to solve conflicts with co-workers - to share conflicts you've experienced at your workplace	· I'm sorry if I... · I think you'd better... · You should try to...	Solving Conflicts	22
CASE STUDY	**Changing Company Culture** Task: To analyze current company culture and bring about positive change.			26

Unit 2. Socializing

Lesson Title	Learning Objectives	Language Practice	Business Basics	Page
Lesson 05 **Business Small Talk**	- to recognize appropriate topics for business small talk - to practice business small talk	· Is this your first time (in)...? · ...is know for its... · Do you...often?	Right Topics for Small Talks	28
Lesson 06 **Business Lunches**	- to understand business lunch etiquette - to explore cross-cultural differences in business luncheons	· I was busy...ing · My pleasure to... · I'd better...	Different Lunch Cultures	32
Lesson 07 **Formal & Informal Communication**	- to understand difference between formal/informal communication - to practice formal/informal communication in business settings	· I was wondering if...? · Do you mind if I...? · I'm not sure if...	Communication Styles	36
Lesson 08 **Online Communication**	- to explore different types of online communication - to talk about the positive/negative effects of online communication	· Let's start with... · It's hard for me to... · I like...ing	Internet Terms	40
CASE STUDY	**Understanding Cultural Differences** Task: To review and understand cultural differences in business lunch norms. Plan to avoid making cultural mistakes.			44

Unit 3. Meetings & Discussions

Lesson Title	Learning Objectives	Language Practice	Business Basics	Page
Lesson 09 **Meeting Preparation**	- to talk about the preparation process for a meeting - to be able to announce meeting information in a formal e-mail	· Plan to… · Keep in mind that… · It has been…since…	Sending Out Formal E-mails	46
Lesson 10 **Opening & Brainstorming**	- to give ideas when brainstorming - to learn ways to effectively communicate with co-workers when brainstorming for ideas	· It seems that… · …better than… · Let me finish…	Mind-mapping	50
Lesson 11 **Conducting Meetings**	- to preside meetings smoothly - to discuss ways to share ideas in a meeting	· Whose…is it? · We'll…next time. · …is joining us today.	Different Meeting Cultures	54
Lesson 12 **Sharing Ideas**	- to express different opinions - to discuss ways to positively share ideas	· Perhaps we should think about… · Are you saying that…? · Speaking of…	Positive Idea Sharing	58
CASE STUDY	Business Problem Solving Task: To create solutions and brainstorm possible consequences for different business problems.			62

Unit 4. Business Trips

Lesson Title	Learning Objectives	Language Practice	Business Basics	Page
Lesson 13 **Business Trip Preparations**	- to make reservations for flights and hotel bookings - to arrange meetings abroad	· I'd appreciate it if you could/would… · I'd rather…than… · I have no problem…ing	Preventing Culture Shock	64
Lesson 14 **Traveling Information**	- to inquire about travel information - to ask for directions and use public transportation	· Does this go (to)…? · How long will it take to get to…? · I was told that…	Culture Quiz	68
Lesson 15 **On the Site**	- to order meals, file hotel complaints, and report stolen goods - to discuss cultural table manner and etiquettes	· I'll get back to you by… · I'd like to treat you to… · Is there any…?	Tipping Etiquettes and Business Dining Manners	72
Lesson 16 **Follow Up**	- to file a report on a trip - to share traveling experiences	· Is it possible to…? · I appreciate your… · Let me know if…	Follow-up Report	76
CASE STUDY	Business Hospitality Task: To extend an invitation to international business partners for a business dinner according to their individual needs and character.			80

Lesson
01

Welcoming Visitors

Learning Objectives

Upon completion of this lesson, you will be able to...

» greet and guide visitors to your company
» introduce yourself, the company and your colleagues

1 Getting Started

A Let's look at the image.

Describe the image in your own words for at least one minute.

B Discuss the following questions.

- What can you do or say to make a visitor feel welcomed at your company?

- How can you address a person when you meet them for the first time at a business setting?

- How do greetings differ in formal and informal settings?

Good to Know — Common Mistakes

Which is right? Check the answers and explanations in the back of the book.

- Everyone **were/was** convinced that he would win the negotiation.
- I think every person in this room **is/are** happy.
- Everybody **have/has** memories of their first love.

2 Language Practice

A Business Expressions
Read the expressions and write your own sentence using the expression.

go the extra mile : to do more than one is required to do to reach a goal.
Ex) *I like doing business with that company; they always go the extra mile.*
Make your own: _____

back to square one : if you are back to square one, you have to start working on a plan from the beginning.
Ex) *I thought everything was settled, but now my clients say they're not happy with the deal, so I'm back to square one.*
Make your own: _____

take matters into your own hands : to deal with a problem yourself because the people who should have dealt with it have failed to do so.
Ex) *Because Nick wasn't able to finish the project on time, his boss decided to take matters into his own hands.*
Make your own: _____

B Key Patterns
Here are some key patterns that you can use when welcoming visitors or as a visitor.

I'm in charge of...	Allow me to...	Could you direct me to...?
• the R&D department	• direct you to the waiting area	• the HR office
• product marketing and advertising	• confirm your appointment	• the nearest restroom
• the international cooperation team	• pass on your details	• the manager of this department

3 Situation & Dialogue

A Answer the following questions using the information given below.

01 Look at the characters and describe the situation.
02 What is the relationship between the characters?
03 What do you think will happen next?

Mr. Andes | In charge of the marketing department of Speed Telecom. Company
MISSION
Ask Mr. Smith who he is looking for and introduce Mr. Smith to Mr. Jones, the new CTO of the company.

Mr. Smith | An investor of Speed Telecom. Company
MISSION
When Mr. Andes asks why you're here, tell him you're here for a business meeting.

Mr. Jones | The new CTO of Speed Telecom. Company.
MISSION
Introduce yourself to Mr. Smith, an investor before starting a meeting.

Quote of the Day!

"A business that makes nothing but money is a poor business."
— Henry Ford

"There are no secrets to success. It is the result of preparation, hard work, and learning from failure."
— Colin Powell

✓ What does success mean to you?
✓ What do you think are the "must-have qualities" to be successful? Make a list and share.
✓ Do you think money always follows success? Why or why not?

B. Practice the dialogue with your partner.

🎧 Welcome to Our Company

Mr. Andes: Hello. You seem to be a visitor; could you tell me who you're looking for?

Mr. Smith: Yes, I'm here for a business meeting with Mr. Andes of the marketing department.

Mr. Andes: Oh that would be me, and you must be Mr. Smith. You're here a little early for our meeting. That's okay. Would you mind following me this way?

Mr. Smith: No, not at all.

Mr. Andes: Did you have any problems finding our company?

Mr. Smith: No, it was quite easy to find.

Mr. Andes: Great. Now let me properly introduce myself. I'm John Andes and I'm in charge of the marketing department here. It's a pleasure to meet you. I would also like to introduce you to our new CTO, Mr. Jones. Mr. Jones, this is Mr. Smith, one of our investors.

Mr. Jones: Very nice to meet you Mr. Smith. I want to thank you for taking your time to visit our company. I hope today's meeting produces positive outcomes.

C. Comprehension Questions

01 | What are some questions you can ask to make your visitor feel comfortable?

02 | What is some important information to include when introducing somebody?

03 | Imagine you are Mr. Jones, the CTO of the company. What can you say to greet and welcome Mr. Smith?

4 Case Scenarios

Read the scenarios and complete each stage.

✓ Scene 1 | Scene 2

A professionally dressed man walks into your office. You think he is a visitor but you're not sure. Ask him why he's here and who he's looking for. Greet the visitor and make him feel welcomed. Then guide him to the meeting area. Introduce yourself and tell him what you are in charge of.

Role A | Employee   **Role B** | Visitor

Scene 1 | ✓ Scene 2

An important business partner visits your company for the first time. Guide your partner to the meeting area. Introduce yourself, the company, and your team members. Then introduce the visitor to everyone else.

Role A | Employee   **Role B** | Visitor

01 Stage
Brainstorm the mission of each character.

» Role A | Mission

» Role B | Mission

02 Stage
How would you feel in each character's position? Explain.

03 Stage
Act out the situation. Make sure to complete the mission of each character and use the key patterns.

Lesson 01 / Welcoming Visitors

5 Business Basics

A Cross Cultural Greetings

Greetings are crucial for leaving positive first impressions. Methods and styles of greeting vary greatly around the world, and you need to know which practices apply in different circumstances.

Country	Greetings	How They Greet
Arab countries	• As-salaam (Peace be upon you) • Sabah el-khair (Good morning) • Masa' el-khair (Good evening)	They shake hands with the right hand only, for longer but less firmly than in the West. Contact between the opposite genders in public is considered obscene. Do not offer to shake hands with the opposite sex.
Philippines	• Magandang umaga (Good morning) • Magandang hapon (Good afternoon)	English is widely spoken in the Philippines. English greetings are also accepted.
China	• Nǐ hǎo (Mandarin greeting)	In formal greetings, oldest person is always greeted first. Handshakes are the most common form of greeting with foreigners.
India	• Namaste ("I bow to divine you")	Greeting your Indian business colleagues with a "namaste" is considered a compliment. It sets the right tone for the rest of your meeting and shows that you've taken time to understand Indian exchanges.
Spain	• Hola, como esta? (Hello, how are you?)	Most Latinos are more accustomed to physical contact. Even people who know each other only slightly may embrace when greeting.

B Share Your Thoughts

01 » Try practicing each countries' greetings with your partner

02 » Imagine your partner is from abroad. Explain your country's greeting. What is it? How do you say it? What gesture do you make?

03 » Do you know any other greetings from a different culture? What do you think these different cultural greetings tell about each country?

Brain Food

In general people shake hands when they meet for a business; however, knowing different cultural greetings may succeed in the international business world. So let's try to keep an open mind.

Review Share 3 things you learned from this lesson

💡 Sneak Peek

01 Do you have a comfortable relationship with your boss? What do you call your boss?

02 Have you been transferred to a different department before?

Lesson 02

Organizational Structure

Learning Objectives

Upon completion of this lesson, you will be able to...

» understand and discuss different organizational structures of companies
» discuss roles and responsibilities of different departments

1 Getting Started

A Let's look at the image.

Describe the image in your own words for at least one minute.

B Discuss the following questions.

- In western countries, subordinates call their bosses by their first names. In your country, what do you call your boss? How would your boss react if you called him or her by their first name?

- What are some elements that show the hierarchical structure of your company? (e.g. desk arrangements, titles, etc)

- If you could be transferred to another department, which department would you want to be transferred to? Why?

Good to Know — Common Mistakes

Which is right? Check the answers and explanations in the back of the book.

Bored vs. Boring

- The movie was so **bored/boring**, I kept falling asleep.
- This book is so **bored/boring**, I'm not going to read it anymore.
- The students got **bored/boring** of studying, so they went to play outside.

2 Language Practice

A Business Expressions
Read the expressions and write your own sentence using the expression.

in a nutshell : to briefly summarize something.
Ex) *She explained the matter to us in a nutshell.*
Make your own: _____

get down to business : to begin to get serious; to get down to work.
Ex) *Now that the contract has been signed, it's time to get down to business.*
Make your own: _____

take the floor : to follow someone else in conducting a meeting or presentation.
Ex) *After John finishes presenting the sales reports, I will take the floor.*
Make your own: _____

B Key Patterns
Here are some key patterns that you can use when discussing organizational structure.

I suspect that…	I might as well…	Have you heard about …?
• I'll be transferred to another team • he'll get promoted this year • my boss will retire soon	• resign from my position • get used to my new position • ask to be transferred to an overseas branch	• the reshuffling of our department • the new promotion policy • the new job rotation system

3 Situation & Dialogue

A Answer the following questions using the information given below.

01. Look at the characters and describe the situation.
02. What is the relationship between the characters?
03. What do you think will happen next?

Mr. Mathis | A team leader in the Sales Department
MISSION
Ms. Jenkins, the director of the HR Department tells you that you are being considered for a promotion. Tell Ms. Jenkins about your accomplishments in your current position (such as sales increases.)

Ms. Jenkins | Director of the HR Department
MISSION
Tell Mr. Mathis, a team leader in the Sales Department, that he is being considered for a promotion. Ask Mr. Mathis to tell you about his accomplishments.

Quote of the Day!

"Ants have the most complicated social organization on earth next to humans."
— E. O. Wilson

"In any great organization it is far, far safer to be wrong with the majority than to be right alone."
— John Kenneth Galbraith

✓ Do you think that most companies have natural or unnatural workplace layouts? What makes a workplace a good fit or bad fit for people?

✓ What do you think? In a company, is it better to be wrong with the majority, or to be right and stand alone?

B Practice the dialogue with your partner.

🎧 Considered for Promotion

Ms. Jenkins: Hello, Mr. Mathis. I hope that you didn't have to wait too long.

Mr. Mathis: It was no problem.

Ms. Jenkins: Well, let's get down to business. Have you heard about the staff changes in your department? I suspect that you have heard that your boss is retiring soon.

Mr. Mathis: Yes, I have.

Ms. Jenkins: I might as well let you know that you are being considered for his position. I've asked you here today to find out where you see your future with this company. Is it okay if I ask you to describe your current responsibilities?

Mr. Mathis: Yes, I'd be happy to. Currently, I lead a team of 12 employees. I assign sales goals and delegate tasks within the team.

Ms. Jenkins: Why should we consider you for this promotion?

Mr. Mathis: I feel that my accomplishments within my department make me an excellent choice for this position. My team has consistently exceeded their quarterly goals and sales volume has increased 12% since I took over as team leader.

Ms. Jenkins: That is quite impressive. What are your future career goals?

Mr. Mathis: I hope to be able to retire in a senior management level position.

C Comprehension Questions

01 | Why did Ms. Jenkins ask Mr. Mathis to come to her office?

02 | What are some of Mr. Mathis' accomplishments?

03 | Imagine you are Mr. Mathis. How would you describe your current responsibilities and career goals?

4 Case Scenarios

Read the scenarios and complete each stage.

   **Role A** | Employee   **Role B** | Supervisor

Your supervisor calls you in to tell you some good news. You have been promoted from assistant manager to section head, because of your excellent leadership skills and your team's good performance in the last quarter. Accept the promotion and ask questions about your new responsibilities.

   **Role A** | HR Manager   **Role B** | Employee

Your company has recently been restructuring. Some employees are being transferred to different departments. You are currently working for the advertising team, but the HR manager calls you in for a meeting to ask you which department you would prefer to be transferred to. You have a choice between the international cooperation team, the marketing team, and the customer support team. Decide which department you want to be transferred to and explain your reason.

 Brainstorm the mission of each character.

>> **Role A | Mission**

>> **Role B | Mission**

 How would you feel in each character's position? Explain.

 Act out the situation. Make sure to complete the mission of each character and use the key patterns.

Lesson 02 / Organizational Structure   17

5 Business Basics

A Do you know hot desking?

Hot desking is where no worker has her or his own fixed personal space. Instead of a permanent desk, each worker must find a new desk each day based on that day's work and co-workers. Possibly, workers could change workplaces throughout the day according to needs and the resources of that work station or area.

B Share Your Thoughts

01 >> Some employees think hot desking is a great idea because it gives them more flexibility to work. On the other hand, some employees find it inconvenient. What do you think are the pros and cons of hot desking? List some pros and cons.

Pros
1.
2.
3.

Cons
1.
2.
3.

Brain Food

Some employees consider themselves 'nesters', and they find it easier to get through long day in work zone that feels like 'their own nest'. By having the comfort and familiarity of a personal space, some workers feel that coming to work is more pleasurable and less jarring.

02 >> Share your list with your partner. Then discuss if you'd like to implement hot desking at your company or not.

03 >> What other types of work environment have you seen other than hot desking?

Review   Share 3 things you learned from this lesson

💡 Sneak Peek

01 What qualities make a co-worker great for collaboration?
02 Could you tell a story about a successful collaboration?

Lesson 03

Collaborating with Co-workers

Learning Objectives

Upon completion of this lesson, you will be able to...
» discuss various ways to get along positively with co-workers
» talk about different working relationships

1 Getting Started

A Let's look at the image.

Describe the image in your own words for at least one minute.

B Discuss the following questions.

- What are some challenges that you face when collaborating with co-workers?
- What do you do when you don't like certain co-workers?
- What is the difference between cooperation and collaboration?

Good to Know — Common Mistakes

Which is right? Check the answers and explanations in the back of the book.

Who vs. Whom
- I don't know to **who/whom** you are speaking.
- **Who/Whom** did you invite to the party?
- With **who/whom** are you discussing the new business proposal?

Lesson 03 / Collaborating with Co-workers

2 Language Practice

A Business Expressions
Read the expressions and write your own sentence using the expression.

hold all the aces : to be in control of everything.
Ex) We are holding all the aces in this negotiation.
Make your own: _____

to buy time : to do something in order to have more time.
Ex) James tried to buy time by telling his boss that he was sick.
Make your own: _____

blank check : a check that has been signed, but does not have the amount of money written in on it.
Ex) His approval on the project is as good as getting a blank check.
Make your own: _____

B Key Patterns
Here are some key patterns that you can use when collaborating with co-workers.

What do you think about...?	I can't stand...	Would you mind if...?
• meeting in the morning • taking a break • stopping for lunch	• working with him • team presentations • our new project	• I left early • I took a break • we continued tomorrow

3 Situation & Dialogue

A Answer the following questions using the information given below.

01 Look at the characters and describe the situation.
02 What is the relationship between the characters?
03 What do you think will happen next?

Ms. Jameson | A new member of the Sales Team who is responsible for making the PowerPoint for an upcoming sales presentation.
MISSION
Ask questions to clarify what the other team members want.

Mr. Blazer | A team leader who is in charge of the presentation.
MISSION
Give suggestion to Ms. Jameson to change an unclear slide. Tell her to add a slide with next quarter's sales targets

Mr. Gupta | A senior team member who will be presenting the data.
MISSION
Offer constructive feedback to Ms. Jameson about the color scheme of her graph and ask her to e-mail you a copy of the presentation.

Quote of the Day!

"Many ideas grow better when transplanted into another mind than the one where they sprang up."
— Oliver Wendell Holmes

"If you have an apple and I have an apple and we exchange these apples then you and I will still each have one apple. But if you have an idea and I have an idea and we exchange these ideas, then each of us will have two ideas."
— George Bernard Shaw

✓ How do you feel about sharing ideas? How do you feel about receiving ideas from others?

✓ Do you think that some people are better at generating ideas and that others are better at putting them into action?

B Practice the dialogue with your partner.

🌐 Collaboration Project

Mr. Blazer:	Hello, Ms. Jameson. We came by to check on how you are doing on the PowerPoint. Would you mind if we took a look at what you've finished so far?
Ms. Jameson:	Of course not. It's my first time doing this, so I'd really appreciate your feedback.
Mr. Blazer:	Overall, everything looks good, but this slide is a little unclear. What do you think, Mr. Gupta?
Mr. Gupta:	I agree…what do you think about changing the color scheme of the graph? The organization is great, but it's a little hard to read.
Ms. Jameson:	What did you have in mind?
Mr. Gupta:	Maybe lighter colors would be better. It's a little bright. Personally, I can't stand bright colors, so maybe I'm biased.
Ms. Jameson:	I think I understand. Just a second….how about this?
Mr. Blazer:	That looks much better. I think you're almost finished. Just make a slide with next quarter's sales targets and I think you are finished. Do you have anything to add, Mr. Gupta?
Mr. Gupta:	No, I think that everything looks great. Thank you for your hard work, Ms. Jameson. Please e-mail me a copy when you are done, so I can start to practice.

C Comprehension Questions

01 | What did Mr. Gupta suggest to Ms. Jameson?
02 | What does Ms. Jameson have to do to finish the presentation?
03 | Have you ever had a team project? What are some challenges and benefits of team projects?

4 Case Scenarios

Read the scenarios and complete each stage.

Scene 1

Your team is preparing a luncheon event for current clients from Germany. You and a team member are responsible for arranging the location and the food for the event, but you have different ideas about what would be best. Your co-worker wants to hold the luncheon at a hotel, but you know a restaurant that you feel would be better.

Role A | Team Member 1
Role B | Team Member 2

Scene 2

You and a co-worker have been asked to work together to write a report summarizing your team's goals for the next quarter. It seems that you will have to work late. Your co-worker seems upset and confesses that today is his/her grandmother's 70th birthday and that he/she doesn't want to miss dinner with his/her family. Your co-worker wants to know if it's okay to meet in the morning before work to finish the report.

Role A | Co-worker 1
Role B | Co-worker 2

 **Stage** Brainstorm the mission of each character.

» **Role A | Mission**

» **Role B | Mission**

 Stage How would you feel in each character's position? Explain.

 **Stage** Act out the situation. Make sure to complete the mission of each character and use the key patterns.

5 Business Basics

A Great Business Partners

The business world brings us into contact with many types of clients and colleagues. While we must get along with everyone if possible, the reality is that each of us has preferences and some relationships work better than others. It is important to consider what type of people are the best co-workers for hiring, matching on projects, and for overall unity and diversity. What are some qualities that you look for in a business partner?

Michale Passafume
Age | 32

Brad Hicks
Age | 34

Personality

Outspoken	Not afraid to voice opinions and criticism; sometimes too critical.
Leadership	In tough times, he is able to provide leadership.
Driven	Refuses to accept failure, and takes pride in professional work.

Personality

Social	Gets along well with many types of people and is complementary.
Daring	Can be a risk taker; however, if things fail, he does not seem to be worried about the consequences.
Humorous	Can use humor to lighten a situation; sometimes not serious enough.

B Share Your Thoughts

01 >> Based on the two people's profile, who would you rather work with? Explain.

02 >> Now create your own 'ideal' co-worker. Write a description of that person by using five characteristics. Share your list with a partner.

03 >> Do you think your co-workers consider you to be a good partner? Why or why not?

Brain Food

An effective way to make a connection with famous people in the industry outside of your company is to invite them to speak at your company's event. That way, you get to make a personal connection and learn from them. Just such an invitation might be the start to a new working relationship and collaboration.

Review Share 3 things you learned from this lesson

💡 Sneak Peek

01 Do you think that conflicts are a necessary part of the business process? Do you tend to avoid conflict at all cost?

02 Do you have preferred way to deal with conflicts?

Lesson 04

Dealing with Conflicts

Learning Objectives

Upon completion of this lesson, you will be able to...
» explore different ways to solve conflicts with co-workers
» share conflicts you've experienced at your workplace

1 Getting Started

A Let's look at the image.

Describe the image in your own words for at least one minute.

B Discuss the following questions.

- What was the greatest conflict or a challenge you've faced at your workplace?
- How do you usually release your stress?
- Did you ever confront a co-worker about a certain problem you've had with him/her? What's the best way to confront someone about a problem?

Good to Know — Common Mistakes

Which is right? Check the answers and explanations in the back of the book.

Affect vs. Effect

- The new law against smoking in restaurants went into **affect/effect** yesterday.
- The president's speech truly **affected/effected** me; I want to serve my country even more.
- What you do now will **affect/effect** your future.

Lesson 04 / Dealing with Conflicts

2 Language Practice

A Business Expressions
Read the expressions and write your own sentence using the expression.

dog-eat-dog : used to describe a situation in which people will do anything to be successful.
Ex) It's a dog-eat-dog world out there, some people will even betray a friend to succeed.
Make your own: _____

at all costs : no matter the risks or difficulties.
Ex) We have to finish this report tonight at all costs.
Make your own: _____

get on the good side of : to win someone's approval.
Ex) Jack wants to get promoted, so he's been trying his hardest to get on the good side of our boss.
Make your own: _____

B Key Patterns
Here are some key patterns that you can use when dealing with conflicts.

I'm sorry if I...	I think you'd better...	You should try to...
• was rude • offended you • misunderstood	• think about this before you talk to him • take a break • calm down	• relax • talk to him • confront him

3 Situation & Dialogue

A Answer the following questions using the information given below.

① Look at the characters and describe the situation.
② What is the relationship between the characters?
③ What do you think will happen next?

Mr. Jones | A member of the HR Department.
MISSION
Discuss Mr. Roger's recent argument with a co-worker, Bill Smith. Listen carefully and try to calm him down, so that he can meet together with Mr. Smith to discuss their problem.

Mr. Rogers | A junior accountant.
MISSION
You are very upset. Tell Mr. Jones about how your co-worker Bill Smith insulted you and the quality of your work when you were paired together for a stressful project.

Quote of the Day!

"Unless both sides win, no agreement can be permanent."
— Jimmy Carter

"Cooperation means win-win, confrontation means lose-lose."
— Zhu Feng

✓ Do you think confrontation is always bad? Isn't it possible to get what you want and deserve by speaking up and challenging people?

✓ Does cooperation always result in a win-win situation?

B Practice the dialogue with your partner.

Solving Conflicts

Mr. Jones: Hello, Mr. Rogers. How are you doing today?

Mr. Rogers: Not very well, but I think you already knew that.

Mr. Jones: I'm sorry to hear that. Would you like to talk about your disagreement with Mr. Smith? I think you'd better start from the beginning and tell me exactly what happened.

Mr. Rogers: It wasn't my fault. He insulted me; he told me that I was disorganized and that he felt that he was doing all the work by himself.

Mr. Jones: Do you think that is true?

Mr. Rogers: Absolutely not. How can you ask me that?

Mr. Jones: I'm sorry if I upset you. I think you know that everyone thinks you are doing a great job. Mr. Smith just reacted badly to a stressful situation. I spoke to him and he feels very sorry about how he spoke to you earlier.

Mr. Rogers: Did he really say that?

Mr. Jones: Yes, he did. I'm going to call him in for a meeting. I think you should try to calmly tell him how those comments made you feel.

C Comprehension Questions

01 | What was the meeting about?

02 | How did Mr. Smith feel after his disagreement with Mr. Rogers?

03 | Imagine that you are Mr. Rogers. What would you want to say to Mr. Jones?

4 Case Scenarios

Read the scenarios and complete each stage.

Scene 1

You are a supervisor in the Marketing department. One of your new team members has come to you with a problem. Your employee feels that another team member is taking advantage of their new status and forcing them to do most of the work on monthly reports. The employee is embarrassed asking for help, but wants to make you aware of the situation.

Role A | Supervisor   **Role B** | New Employee

Scene 2

You have been at your company for two years. Recently, you have been assigned a big project and as a result, your workload has nearly doubled. You feel that you have no personal time and are feeling very stressed. You are unsure how much longer you will be able to keep working in your position. You have a very close relationship with your team leader. Ask for advice on how to manage your stress and workload.

Role A | Employee   **Role B** | Team Leader

01 Stage Brainstorm the mission of each character.

>> **Role A | Mission**

>> **Role B | Mission**

02 Stage How would you feel in each character's position? Explain.

03 Stage Act out the situation. Make sure to complete the mission of each character and use the key patterns.

Lesson 04 / Dealing with Conflicts

5 Business Basics

A Solving Conflicts

For better or worse, conflicts are a part of business life. Learning how to manage conflicts can help determine your business success. You can try different tactics such as conflict prevention or mitigation. Secondly, you could have a process ready in order to address such disputes. However, essentially, people need to have understanding and willpower to overcome such obstacles.

Conflict Two co-workers are having a dispute. Jane is very shy and has a passive personality. James accuses Jane of not giving enough of her ideas in meetings. James thinks that Jane is intentionally keeping quiet because she's not interested or doesn't like James.

Solution:

B Share Your Thoughts

01 Read the conflict between James and Jane. Then come up with a positive solution to resolve the conflict. Then share your answer with a partner.

02 If you were James what would you do? If you were Jane, what would you do?

03 Did you ever consider resigning because of a conflict at your company?

Brain Food

WIIFM is an acronym for: 'What's In It For Me?' In English, this phrase means how does a thing or action benefit me? In a conflict, each side has a motive for their position. By understanding the other side's interest and objective, you can have the knowledge to move closer to a workable resolution.

Review Share 3 things you learned from this lesson

💡 Sneak Peek

01 When do you usually use small talk?

02 What are some topics you use for small talk?

Business Basics 1

01 Changing Company Culture

◉ Background

Dionte Baudin just relocated from the main corporate office to an overseas branch office. Up until now, the overseas office operated according to their own plans and policies. However Dionte's quest is to adjust the overseas' office to create a different and more loyal workforce.

◉ Tasks

Take a look below at the current culture in the overseas branch and some of Dionte's ideas to change the culture.

Current Work Culture	New Work Culture Ideas
· Strict hierarchical system, employees call their bosses using titles.	· To create a more relaxed work environment, all staffs should call each other using first names.
· There is a gym in the same building, but employees must pay to use it.	· Free gym membership for employees.
· No lounge or rest area. No free drinks.	·
· Some working moms have difficulty managing work and housework.	·
· Many employees are from different countries and have difficulty communicating with each other.	·
· No bonus program in effect.	·
· No 'creative time' is built into the work schedule.	·
· The company does believe in charity, but the company volunteers together four times a year on Saturday. Workers are not compensated but the company pays for lunch.	

01 Now, add to Dionte's list of ideas to make the work place better. Write down your ideas in the chart.

02 Next, Dionte wants to hold a meeting regarding his new ideas to improve the workplace. He wants to hear what employees have to say and at the same time propose changes. Help him brainstorm for the meeting by filling in the chart below.

CASE STUDY 01

Dionte's Meeting Ideas

✓ Subject/Purpose:

✓ Date:

✓ Participants:

Agenda Item	Decision	Reason	Action
1. Using first names	Currently, there is a strict hierarchical system; staff can start to use first names to create a more relaxed atmosphere.	Addressing each other by first names will create the sense of equality and ease the tension.	All staff should use first names.
2.			
3.			
4.			

03 Finally, compare your ideas with your partner. Decide whether you agree or disagree with your partner's decision.

Agenda	Agree	Disagree
1.		
2.		
3.		
4.		

Lesson 05

Business Small Talk

Learning Objectives

Upon completion of this lesson, you will be able to...
» recognize appropriate topics for business small talk
» practice business small talk

1 Getting Started

A Let's look at the image.

Describe the image in your own words for at least one minute.

B Discuss the following questions.

- What are some topics you can use for small talk?
- Do you feel comfortable/uncomfortable when there is silence? Why or why not?
- What are some topics/questions considered inappropriate for small talk?

Good to Know — Common Mistakes

Which is right? Check the answers and explanations in the back of the book.

Farther vs. Further

- We should discuss this topic **farther/further**.
- **Farther/Further** input from all the groups is needed to make the best decision.
- I live **farther/further** outside of the city than you do.

Lesson 05 / Business Small Talk

2 Language Practice

A Business Expressions
Read the expressions and write your own sentence using the expression.

finger in every pie : to be involved in many different activities. (often negative)
Ex) *John seems to know everything, he really has a finger in every pie in this office.*
Make your own: _____

donkey work : the hard, boring part of a job.
Ex) *I think I made a mistake doing the easy part first. Now I'm stuck doing the donkey work.*
Make your own: _____

long haul : long distance; long-term.
Ex) *I just came back from my business trip and now I feel exhausted after my long haul flight.*
Make your own: _____

B Key Patterns
Here are some key patterns that you can use when making small talk with others.

Is this your first time (in)...?	...is known for its...	Do you...often?
• London • visiting our office • working with us	• Seattle...coffee • This restaurant...pasta • Our city...architecture	• travel for work • come here • do business here

3 Situation & Dialogue

A Answer the following questions using the information given below.

01 Look at the characters and describe the situation.
02 What is the relationship between the characters?
03 What do you think will happen next?

Mr. Craig | A Vice President in the Marketing department.
MISSION
Greet clients who are visiting from another city, including Ms. White. Make small talk with her and recommend that she visit Springfield's famous theater district.

Ms. White | A representative from Ace Company.
MISSION
You are visiting your supplier's home office in Springfield for the first time. Make small talk with Mr. Craig while you wait for your meeting to start.

Quote of the Day!

"Talk to anyone about himself and he will listen without interrupting."
— Herber Prochnow

"The time to stop talking is when the other person nods his head affirmatively but says nothing."
— Henry S. Haskins

✓ Who do you talk to the most during the day?

✓ Do you think you're a good listener? or a good conversation leader?

B Practice the dialogue with your partner.

🌐 Making Small Talk

Mr. Craig: Hello, my name is John Craig. I'm the vice president of the marketing department.

Ms. White: Joanna White from Ace Corp. Nice to meet you.

Mr. Craig: Nice to meet you, too. Is this your first time in Springfield?

Ms. White: Yes, it is. I haven't got to see much of it yet. What do you recommend I see here?

Mr. Craig: Do you like plays? Springfield is known for its theater district. If you have time, you should try to watch one.

Ms. White: I love the theater. Do you watch plays often?

Mr. Craig: I used to, but not very much lately.

Ms. White: Oh…I think it's time to go in for the meeting. It was very nice to meet you, Mr. Craig.

Mr. Craig: I enjoyed talking to you Ms. White. I'll see you inside the meeting.

C Comprehension Questions

01 | What does Mr. Craig recommend for Ms. White?

02 | Why do they stop talking?

03 | Imagine you are making small talk with a visitor to your city. What would you recommend they see?

4 Case Scenarios

Read the scenarios and complete each stage.

Scene 1

Role A Employee
Role B Client

Several out-of-town clients have come to your office today to listen to a presentation. Traffic was unusually bad, so your boss is running a little late. You need to entertain the clients for about 10 minutes until your boss arrives to start the presentation. Offer them coffee and ask about their visit so far.

Scene 2

Role A Overseas Visitor
Role B Employee

You are responsible for taking some overseas clients from the airport to their hotel. It is their first trip to your country. Pass time in the car by asking them about their interests and recommending some tourist attractions for them to see in your city.

01 Stage | Brainstorm the mission of each character.

» **Role A | Mission**

» **Role B | Mission**

02 Stage | How would you feel in each character's position? Explain.

03 Stage | Act out the situation. Make sure to complete the mission of each character and use the key patterns.

5 Business Basics

A Small Talk

Small talk can be crucial to getting off to a good start with a person. However, the wrong small talk can leave a lasting negative impression that could damage any chance at a future relationship. When meeting people across cultures, it is imperative to be sensitive to which topics will interest them and which will disturb them. Also, it is good to be mindful of the different expectations that each culture has regarding small talk.

B Share Your Thoughts

01 >> Look at the list of small talk topics below. Select which ones are appropriate and explain why the others are not appropriate. Share your answer with a partner.

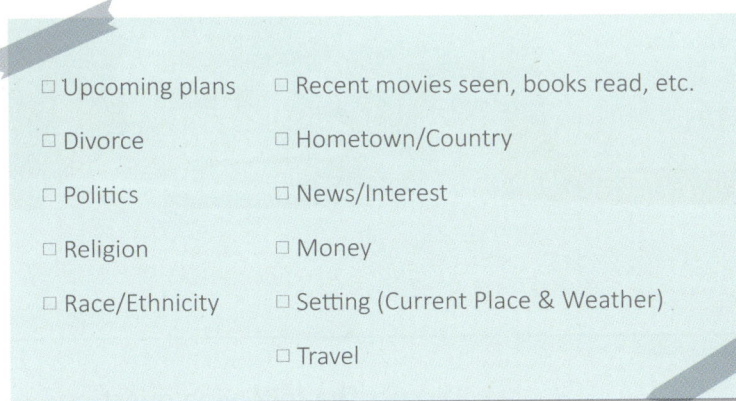

- ☐ Upcoming plans
- ☐ Divorce
- ☐ Politics
- ☐ Religion
- ☐ Race/Ethnicity
- ☐ Recent movies seen, books read, etc.
- ☐ Hometown/Country
- ☐ News/Interest
- ☐ Money
- ☐ Setting (Current Place & Weather)
- ☐ Travel

Brain Food

Supposedly, the best way to get a conversation going is to get the other person to talk positively about himself/herself. The idea is that people love talking about themselves and therefore would be happy to do so. As long as you are a good and patient listener, this tactic could be one way to get through the small talk.

02 >> What are some topics you do not want to discuss for small talk?

03 >> When's the best time for small talk?

Review   Share 3 things you learned from this lesson

💡 Sneak Peek

01 Some people enjoy power lunches. In a power lunch, you discuss actual business and make deals. How do you feel about mixing business and dining?

02 Some people eat alone because they like to use lunch time as private time to think. What is your view on eating alone?

Lesson 06

Business Lunches

Learning Objectives
Upon completion of this lesson, you will be able to...
» to understand business lunch etiquette
» explore cross-cultural differences in business luncheons

1 Getting Started

A Let's look at the image.

Describe the image in your own words for at least one minute.

B Discuss the following questions.

- What are some basic examples of table etiquette?
- What do you consider the most important thing to keep in mind when eating lunch with a client/business partner/boss?
- Exchange 3 small talk questions with your partner.

Good to Know — Common Mistakes

Which is right? Check the answers and explanations in the back of the book.

Then vs. Than
- Today, our team worked longer **then/than** yesterday.
- I will see you tomorrow **then/than**, right?
- Some countries are more prosperous **then/than** other countries.

2 Language Practice

A Business Expressions
Read the expressions and write your own sentence using the expression.

to jump the gun : to do something too soon without thinking carefully about it.
Ex) We really jumped the gun agreeing to the terms of this deal. I feel like we didn't read the contract carefully enough.
Make your own: _____

on the house : complementary; to be given something by a business.
Ex) Because you have always been such good customers, dinner is on the house tonight.
Make your own: _____

go Dutch : to split the cost of something, especially a meal.
Ex) Do you want to go Dutch on dinner? I'm a little short on cash.
Make your own: _____

B Key Patterns
Here are some key patterns that you can use while having business lunch.

I was busy ...ing	My pleasure to...	I'd better...
• talking on the phone	• meet you here	• order dessert
• driving when you called	• take you to lunch	• buy you coffee
• parking my car	• share a meal with you	• thank you for coming

3 Situation & Dialogue

A Answer the following questions using the information given below.

01 Look at the characters and describe the situation.
02 What is the relationship between the characters?
03 What do you think will happen next?

Ms. Jackson | A sales representative having lunch with Mr. Friedman.
MISSION
Thank Mr. Friedman for meeting you and explain that you have already ordered.

Mr. Friedman | An executive who is engaged in a business partnership with Ms. Jackson's company.
MISSION
Explain you were late because you were parking your car. Then, order something to drink.

Waiter | An employee of the restaurant.
MISSION
Take Mr. Friedman's drink order and ask Ms. Jackson if she wants anything.

Quote of the Day!

"One cannot think well, love well, sleep well, if one has not dined well."
— Virginia Woolf

"The discovery of a new dish does more for the happiness of the human race than the discovery of a star."
— Jean Anthelme Brillat-Savarin

✓ Do you think that sharing food can help people overcome cultural differences?
✓ How do you use lunch/dinner with a business partner for the benefit of your company?

B Practice the dialogue with your partner.

🎧 Lunch With a Business Partner

Mr. Friedman: Hello, Ms. Jackson. I hope you didn't wait too long. I was busy parking when you called.

Ms. Jackson: Not at all. My pleasure to meet you here. Was it difficult to find the restaurant?

Mr. Friedman: No, it was quite easy. You gave me excellent directions.

Ms. Jackson: I hope you don't mind, but I went ahead and ordered us the chef's special.

Mr. Friedman: It looks delicious.

Ms. Jackson: Would you like anything else? I see the waiter coming by.

Mr. Friedman: I'd better get something to drink. Do you want anything, Ms. Jackson?

Waiter: How may I help you?

Mr. Friedman: I'd like an iced tea with lemon.

Waiter: Anything for you, ma'am?

Ms. Jackson: No, thank you. I'm fine.

Waiter: I'll be right back with your drink, sir.

C Comprehension Questions

01 | Why did Mr. Friedman miss Ms. Jackson's call?

02 | Based on the dialogue, who do you think is the person that made the invitation?

03 | What are some things you consider important when having meals with a business partner?

4 Case Scenarios

Read the scenarios and complete each stage.

Situation 1

You work at Ace Computers and your company has a long-standing relationship with EElect Manufacturing. A new representative from this company has been assigned to work with you. You want to get to know your new business partner a little better by inviting them to lunch. Ask what kind of restaurant they enjoy and suggest a place to meet. Work out a time and a date to meet with your partner.

Role A
Marketing representative of Ace Computer

Role B
Representative from Elect Manufacturing

Situation 2

Your company, Ace Computers is hosting a business luncheon for their clients. You are sitting next to a client that you have worked with a lot in the past. You know them well from work and want to get to know more about them on a personal level. Discuss the food and make small talk about their family and interests.

Role A Employee of Ace Computers
Role B Client of Ace Computers

01 Stage Brainstorm the mission of each character.

» **Role A | Mission**

» **Role B | Mission**

02 Stage How would you feel in each character's position? Explain.

03 Stage Act out the situation. Make sure to complete the mission of each character and use the key patterns.

5 Business Basics

A Table Manners

Having good table manners and etiquette shows sensitivity to detail and treatment of others. Table manners are a good part of hospitality as well as being accepted as a guest. Thus, it is valuable to know and practice good manners. However, the challenge is that even with globalization, a universal set of table manners still does not quite exist. Have you ever encountered difficulties when dining abroad?

Korean Dining Etiquette

- Sometimes the eating of noodles requires 'slurping' or the pulling in of long noodles.
- Some sounds could show satisfaction with the meal.
- Sitting on the floor is customary.
- Sharing food from the same serving bowl is very common and indicates friendship and acceptance.

United States Dining Etiquette

- Take small bites whenever possible.
- Try to be as noiseless as possible.
- Sitting at a table with chairs is customary.
- People on rare occasion share food, however, it is by mutual consent with one person offering to share a portion with another. If accepted, one morsel is transferred by spoon or fork.

B Share Your Thoughts

01 >> Looking at the list above, what do you think the lunch etiquette of the two countries tells about eating culture?

02 >> The phrase "go Dutch" indicates that each person pays his or her own bill at a group meal. How do you feel about this practice?

03 >> What are some things you consider the most important when eating out with other people?

Brain Food

Since dining etiquette represents the values and traditions of culture, when dining in another culture it should be a good chance to learn. You can even ask many questions and start conversation. Which dining etiquette best represents your culture?

Review Share 3 things you learned from this lesson

Sneak Peek

01 What is your standard for formal and informal communication?
02 Do you ever use informal communication in a business setting?

Lesson 07

Formal & Informal Communication

Learning Objectives

Upon completion of this lesson, you will be able to...
» understand the difference between formal/informal communication
» practice formal/informal communication in business settings

1 Getting Started

A Let's look at the image.

Describe the image in your own words for at least one minute.

B Discuss the following questions.

- What do you think is the most important factor for good communication?

- What is the difference between talking and speaking?

- When do you use formal communication? Informal communication? Which is more comfortable for you and why?

Common Mistakes

Which is right? Check the answers and explanations in the back of the book.

There vs. Their vs. They're

- **There/Their/They're** were many people in the conference room.
- The analysts reviewed the data in **there/their/they're** budget report.
- In the seminar room, **there/their/they're** setting up for a luncheon.

Lesson 07 / Formal & Informal Communication   37

2 Language Practice

A Business Expressions
Read the expressions and write your own sentence using the expression.

go down the drain : for something to become spoiled or wasted.
Ex) I was so sad when my team's project was cancelled. It was hard to watch all of our hard work go down the drain.
Make your own: _____

second a motion : to agree with a motion that someone has proposed in a meeting.
Ex) I agree with the proposal, so I will second his motion.
Make your own: _____

no brainer : a decision that is very easy.
Ex) Given John's extensive experience, letting him take over the account was a no brainer.
Make your own: _____

B Key Patterns
Here are some key patterns that you can use for formal workplace communication.

I was wondering if...?	Do you mind if I...?	I'm not sure if...
• you had a minute	• call back later	• I can help you
• you could help me	• go to the bathroom	• I understand
• you could talk	• take this phone call	• I have time to talk now

3 Situation & Dialogue

A Answer the following questions using the information given below.

01. Look at the characters and describe the situation.
02. What is the relationship between the characters?
03. What do you think will happen next?

Ms. Tate | A sales representative from Office Supplies, Inc.
MISSION
Warmly greet Mr. Mason. When Mr. Mason tells you his problem, offer your help solving a delivery problem with a recent order.

Mr. Mason | A client of Office Supplies, Inc.
MISSION
Tell Ms. Tate about a problem that you had with the quality of their most recent shipment of paper.

"If you wouldn't write it and sign it, don't say it."
— Earl Wilson

"To speak and to speak well are two things. A fool may talk, but a wise man speaks."
— Ben Jonson

✓ Was there a time where you said something that you shouldn't have?

✓ How do you improve your speaking? Do you try to acquire new vocabulary regularly?

B Practice the dialogue with your partner.

🌐 Talking to a Client: Formal Communication

Ms. Tate: Good morning, Mr. Mason. How are you doing today?

Mr. Mason: I'm fine. And you?

Ms. Tate: I'm doing well. What can I do for you today?

Mr. Mason: There was a problem with our latest shipment of paper. Most of the units had water damage.

Ms. Tate: I'm sorry to hear that. That's a very unusual situation. Would you like to exchange the damaged units?

Mr. Mason: No, I was hoping that you could give me a refund. The situation was really inconvenient.

Ms. Tate: That is a very difficult situation, but I'm not sure if I can refund your purchase. Do you mind if I call my supervisor and check?

Mr. Mason: Not at all. Go right ahead.

Ms. Tate: His line is busy now. I was wondering if it would be okay to call you back tomorrow. I'm not sure about the exact terms of your contract, so I need to confirm before I make any promises.

Mr. Mason: That's fine. Let me know what you can do. Thank you for coming out today.

C Comprehension Questions

01 | What was the problem with the paper shipment?

02 | Why can't Ms. Tate give Mr. Mason an answer today?

03 | Did you ever have to solve a problem with a client? What was the problem? How did you deal with the problem?

4 Case Scenarios

Read the scenarios and complete each stage.

Scene 1

Your colleague has asked you out to lunch at a restaurant near your office. You have worked together for nearly two years and you have a friendly relationship. Make casual conversation about personal interests and recent projects while you eat. While you are at the restaurant, your supervisor walks by your table. He came to the restaurant by coincidence. He asks if it is okay to join you. Your casual conversation now changes to formal talk with your boss.

Casual Conversation **Role A** | Employee 1   **Role B** | Employee 2
Formal Conversation **Role A** | Employee 1   **Role B** | Boss

Scene 2

You have been called into your manager's office. Your manager wants to be updated on a recent project that your team has been working on. The project is going well, but your team is a little behind schedule because one of your team members has quit suddenly. Explain the situation to your boss.

Role A | General Manager   **Role B** | Team Leader

01 Stage | Brainstorm the mission of each character.

» **Role A** | Mission

» **Role B** | Mission

02 Stage | How would you feel in each character's position? Explain.

03 Stage | Act out the situation. Make sure to complete the mission of each character and use the key patterns.

5 Business Basics

A Type of Communication

In business and social life, how we speak to others often determines the results we get. Language represents ourselves and shows how we think about others. Thus, it is important to 'strike the right' tone to fit the situation and relationship of the person being spoken, too. Word choice and language patterns will shape the 'tone and voice' of language.

Different Communication Styles

Formal	Informal	Passive	Aggressive
- Standard English that is grammatically correct	- Substandard English	- Indirect	- Direct
- Avoids slangs and clichés	- Uses slang and improper grammar	- Considered polite	- Could be rude
- Avoids contractions	- Uses contradictions	- Could be too vague or indefinite	- More clear and forceful

B Share Your Thoughts

01 » Read the phrase and check the correct description.

Phrases	Formal	Informal	Passive	Aggressive
I beg your pardon?				
Drink anyone?				
Your idea is good, but I think we should try to come up with another.				
You're wrong.				
Excuse me?				

Speaking passively can be a good way to test out and offer ideas. Also, it is a pleasant way to offer a choice to someone and to defer to their judgment. On the other hand, speaking aggressively can reach a conclusion right away. Also, it can eliminate ambiguity. Try each style according to the situation and your goals.

02 » In East Asian cultures, saying 'No' directly might be considered rude. Sometimes people say yes, even when they really mean no. How do you feel about it?

03 » Are you a passive speaker, or an aggressive speaker?

Review   Share 3 things you learned from this lesson

💡 Sneak Peek

01 Do you think that online communication leaves us with too little privacy?
02 Has online communication made your life more convenient or stressful?

Lesson 08

Online Communication

Learning Objectives

Upon completion of this lesson, you will be able to...
» explore different types of online communication
» talk about the positive/negative effects of online communication

1 Getting Started

A Let's look at the image.

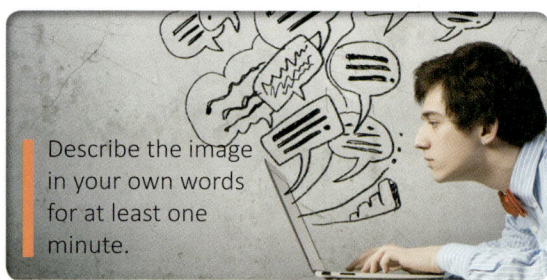

Describe the image in your own words for at least one minute.

B Discuss the following questions.

- Do you use SNS? What do you like and don't like about SNS?
- Does your company utilize online communication? If so, how?
- Some people say face-face meetings are too time consuming, and prefer conference call meetings. What do you think? Which do you prefer?

Good to Know — Common Mistakes

Which is right? Check the answers and explanations in the back of the book.

Complement Vs. Compliment
- The teamwork is great! All of you **complement/compliment** each other.
- Thank you for the **complement/compliment**! Your praise is precious to me.
- The new software suite **complements/compliments** the existing version.

Lesson 08 / Online Communication   41

2 Language Practice

A Business Expressions
Read the expressions and write your own sentence using the expression.

cutting edge : very modern.
Ex) The firm uses a sophisticated software system; they are known for their cutting edge approach to doing business.
Make your own: _____

bottom line : the line in the accounts of a company that states the total profit or loss.
Ex) We need to think about how this purchase will affect our bottom line. It might just put us in debt.
Make your own: _____

no strings attached : when an agreement has no special terms or limits.
Ex) He offered us a great deal on the new computers- no strings attached.
Make your own: _____

B Key Patterns
Here are some key patterns that you can use during online communications, such as conference calls.

Let's start with...	It's hard for me to...	I like...ing
• the sales data • introducing ourselves • going over the meeting agenda	• learn new technology • hear you clearly over the phone • input data in the new program	• using this new SMS system • communicating over the phone • meeting in person rather than e-mailing

3 Situation & Dialogue

A Answer the following questions using the information given below.

01 Look at the characters and describe the situation.
02 What is the relationship between the characters?
03 What do you think will happen next?

Quote of the Day!

"The Internet is just the world passing around notes in a classroom."
— Jon Stewart

"The Internet is becoming the town square for the global village of tomorrow."
— Bill Gates

✓ Do you feel that the Internet is more of a time saver or a time waster? Can you give examples of each?

✓ Do you think people seclude themselves from others due to the internet? or do you think the internet brought people closer?

Mr. Andrews | General Manager of the overseas branch
MISSION
Thank Mr. Black for calling and apologize that he had to come into the office early to make the call because of the time difference. Explain that there is a problem with your conference call system and offer to email Mr. Black the data tomorrow.

Mr. Black | An executive member of the International Cooperation Team
MISSION
Call Mr. Andrews for a scheduled conference call. Ask Mr. Andrews about his branch's quarterly data. When Mr. Andrews tells you that there is a problem with his system, offer to schedule another conference call.

UNIT 2. Socializing

B Practice the dialogue with your partner.

🎧 Conference Call

Mr. Black:	Good evening, Mr. Andrews. How are you doing today?
Mr. Andrews:	I'm doing fine. Thank you so much for calling me. I'm sorry that you had to come in so early to make the call.
Mr. Black:	It was no problem. I like taking the bus early. It's so much more peaceful. Now, why don't we get down to business. Let's start with discussing the quarterly sales data.
Mr. Andrews:	Everything is looking good. From the start of the quarter, our sales volume has increased almost 8%.
Mr. Black:	That's quite an impressive change. Would you mind sending me a copy of your data?
Mr. Andrews:	I'm sorry, but there's something wrong with my conference call system. It's hard for me to hear you. Can you hear me?
Mr. Black:	Yes, I hear you fine.
Mr. Andrews:	The connection keeps getting lost. Would it be okay if I e-mail you the copy of the data by tomorrow morning your time?
Mr. Black:	That will be fine. We can set up another conference call once I get the data to look at.
Mr. Andrews:	I'll e-mail you my schedule in the morning.
Mr. Black:	Okay. Talk to you soon.

C Comprehension Questions

01 | What does Mr. Black want to discuss?

02 | Why can't Mr. Andrews send the data now?

03 | What kinds of technology do you use to communicate in your workplace? What do you use them for?

4 Case Scenarios

Read the scenarios and complete each stage.

Scene 1

Your co-worker is very frustrated with a new computer program and misses communicating the old-fashioned way. You think that modern technology has greatly improved inter-office communication. Discuss the pros and cons of online communication with your co-worker.

Role A
Co-worker 1: Likes using online communication

Role B
Co-worker 2: Doesn't like online communication

Scene 2

Your company has recently purchased a new SNS system. Some people enjoy the speed of communication, but others feel that it makes them less likely to talk to some of their colleagues in person. Your department head has been using it to assign work, which feels very impersonal. One of your co-workers dislikes receiving work assignments via SNS, because s/he thinks short messages are rude. Discuss the problem with your colleague.

Role A
Co-worker 1: Dislikes being assigned work via SNS

Role B
Co-worker 2: Thinks SNS is an efficient mode of communication

01 Stage | Brainstorm the mission of each character.

» **Role A | Mission**

» **Role B | Mission**

02 Stage | How would you feel in each character's position? Explain.

03 Stage | Act out the situation. Make sure to complete the mission of each character and use the key patterns.

5 Business Basics

A Internet Terms

The purpose behind much technology is to save time and to make processes more effective than before. Thus, when using a new format like e-mail, most people do the same basic activity not only with a new device but also in a new way. For example, in writing and communicating, people may write differently (i.e. using abbreviations). This technique, while effective on the one hand, could create confusion in meaning and also seem too informal in certain situations. So let's take a look at several examples.

Abbreviation	Meaning
TTYL	Talk To You Later
TMRW	Tomorrow
PLZ	Please
THX	Thanks
B/C	Because
NVM	Never mind

B Share Your Thoughts

01 Choose at least two abbreviations from the list and write a sentence.

....

....

....

02 Try to remember all the abbreviations from the list. Then test your partner to see if he/she remembers all of them.

03 How do you feel about using emoticons in your message?

Brain Food

Taking advantage of digital communications is crucial for business success. However, because of that, timeless ways of communicating could be more meaningful than ever. For example, inviting people out for a coffee after work could do far more than countless e-mails. Also, the power of a hand-written note to thank or congratulate someone could distinguish you from the rest.

Review   Share 3 things you learned from this lesson

💡 Sneak Peek

01 Why do you usually hold meetings at your company?

02 What are some things you need to check before holding a team meeting?

Business Basics 1

02 Understanding Cultural Differences

Background

If you're traveling abroad on business trips, you may find lunch culture a lot different from yours. Every country has different customs and it may be a good idea to know them beforehand and impress your business partners.

Country	Lunch Time	Lunch Length	Meal	Talking Business
Spain	12:30-4:00	3+ hours	Lunch lasts a long time and business talk starts slow. Enjoying meal and developing relationship is more important.	Late in the meal
Russia	1:00-2:30	1-1.5 hours	There are usually at least three courses to a Russian lunch. Tea or coffee is typically served with lunch; soft drinks and wine are rarely served. It is also quite common to see vodka being consumed with lunch.	Throughout the meal
Scandinavia	12:00-1:00	1 hour	Lunch meal is usually very light. Bread and shrimp are the only foods eaten by hand. Even fruit is eaten with utensils.	Throughout the meal
France	12:00-2:00	2 hours	In France, the main meal is served at lunchtime and a lighter supper is served later. The French like to take a long time over their lunch.	After dessert is served
Your Country				

CASE STUDY 02

◉ Tasks

01 Now, add your country's lunch culture to the list. Which country has the most similar lunch culture? Most different?

02 Imagine you are eating lunch with a business partner from a different country. To avoid awkward silences, you need to start small talk. In the chart below, make a list of small talk topics.

Small Talk Topic	Questions You can Ask

03 Now, imagine your partner is the business partner from abroad. Practice small talk with your partner. Try to have small talk for 3 minutes straight. Time yourself.

✓ Small Talk Checklist

Things to check for...	Yes	No
Did your small talk last for 3 minutes?		
Were your small talk topics appropriate?		
Did you find out any interesting fact about your partner?		
Was your small talk smooth flowing?		
Were your questions appropriate?		

Lesson 09

Meeting Preparation

Learning Objectives

Upon completion of this lesson, you will be able to...
» talk about preparation process for a meeting
» announce meeting information in a formal e-mail

1 Getting Started

A Let's look at the image.

Describe the image in your own words for at least one minute.

B Discuss the following questions.

- What is the most important thing to remember when preparing for a meeting?

- What can you do to increase the participant rate for your meeting?

- In your team meeting, does everyone get an equal chance to speak? Or does your boss do most of the speaking? What can you do to give everyone a fair chance to speak at a meeting?

Good to Know — Common Mistakes

Which is right? Check the answers and explanations in the back of the book.

Lose Vs. Loose

- If you **lose/loose** the bidding competition, then the company will have lower 4th quarter sales.

- New paint and recent improvements to the national monument already had become **lose/loose**, so citizens were angry.

- We need to tie up all the **lose/loose** ends in the business expansion plan.

Lesson 09 / Meeting Preparation

2 Language Practice

A Business Expressions
Read the expressions and write your own sentence using the expression.

make ends meet : to have just enough money to pay for things you need.
Ex) With the economy so bad now, it's really hard to make ends meet these days.
Make your own: _____

put something on hold : to delay until a later time.
Ex) We're going to have to put this project on hold until we can find funding.
Make your own: _____

learn the ropes : to learn how to do a new job or activity.
Ex) Don't worry if things seem hard now. Your job will get easier once you learn the ropes.
Make your own: _____

B Key Patterns
Here are some key patterns that you can use while preparing for meetings.

Plan to...	Keep in mind that...	It has been...since...
• get up early tomorrow • finish this report before the meeting • arrive 15 minutes early for the meeting	• a new client will be attending • you will need to brief the team on your progress • the meeting starts at 9	• two weeks...the last meeting • a week...the meeting plan was set • a long time...we had a team meeting

3 Situation & Dialogue

A Answer the following questions using the information given below.
01 Look at the characters and describe the situation.
02 What is the relationship between the characters?
03 What do you think will happen next?

Mr. Plaza | Team Leader in the Sales department
MISSION
During the team meeting, ask Ms. Malone to update the sales charts and tell Mr. Roberts that he will need to set up the projector in the conference room.

Ms. Malone | Member of Mr. Plaza's Sales team
MISSION
When Mr. Plaza asks you where the sales data are from, tell him they're from last year and that you plan to update them today.

Mr. Roberts | Member of Mr. Plaza's Sales team
MISSION
When Mr. Plaza asks you to set up for the investor's meeting tomorrow ask him how many people will attend the meeting.

Quote of the Day!

"Spectacular achievement is always preceded by unspectacular preparation."
— Robert H. Schuller

"By failing to prepare you are preparing to fail."
— Benjamin Franklin

✓ Was there a time where you didn't prepare at all and ended in a complete success?

✓ Do you think that failure is always connected to lack of preparation?

UNIT 3. Meetings & Discussions

B Practice the dialogue with your partner.

💡 Organization Reshuffle

Mr. Plaza:	Let me take a look at what you two have done so far…it all looks good, but keep in mind that an important investor is attending, so we need to be a little more thorough than usual. Ms. Malone, where did you get these charts from?
Ms. Malone:	I took them from the last report.
Mr. Plaza:	It has been a while since we updated them.
Ms. Malone:	Yes, I know. I plan to update them today.
Mr. Plaza:	We should talk about your roles tomorrow. Ms. Malone, plan to present the data. Mr. Roberts, you know how to set up the projector, right? Could you come in a little early to set up for our investor's meeting tomorrow?
Mr. Roberts:	Yes, of course.
Mr. Plaza:	Good. I think we are about set now. Any questions?
Mr. Roberts:	Do you know how many people will be attending? Last time, we didn't have enough chairs.
Mr. Plaza:	That's a good question. I will confirm and get back to you.

C Comprehension Questions

01 | What will be Mr. Roberts' and Ms. Malone's roles in tomorrow's meeting?

02 | Why did Mr. Roberts ask about chairs?

03 | How often do you have meetings at your workplace? How can you ensure that a meeting is effective?

4 Case Scenarios

Read the scenarios and complete each stage.

Scene 1

Your team leader has instructed you and your partner to write and present your team's progress report at the monthly department meeting. You and your partner decide that it makes more sense to divide the work. Decide on how you will divide the roles and responsibilities for the task, and who will take on each role.

Role A	**Role B**
Team Member 1: Strongly prefers writing the report	Team Member 2: Prefers writing the report, but is willing to present

Scene 2

You are the Manager of Gold Pharmaceutical Company's Sales Division. You want to call a meeting to check the sales teams' progress with selling a new flu vaccine. Call a Team Leader into your office and notify her/him about the time and date of the meeting. Tell the Team Leader s/he should prepare to present sales data for the last quarter.

Role A	**Role B**
Department Manager	Team Leader

01 Stage Brainstorm the mission of each character.

» **Role A | Mission**

» **Role B | Mission**

 02 Stage How would you feel in each character's position? Explain.

 03 Stage Act out the situation. Make sure to complete the mission of each character and use the key patterns.

5 Business Basics

A Addressing Formality

Formality shows deliberateness. Thus, it is a way to show value for your audience, time, and the importance of your message. Formality is a matter of word choice, structure, phrases, and manner to show intent and respect. It is even possible to be a bit humorous, if thoughtfully placed and strictly limited. Think of formality as creating a verbal setting for the proper exchange of ideas. Remember: input often determines output, so how you write reflects what type of response you might get.

B Share Your Thoughts

Read the e-mail below.

Hey team members!

How are you? As usual, we'll be getting together for our regular meeting tomorrow at 2 p.m. Everybody can make it, right? Don't be late. Bring all your topics and concerns to meeting. We will deal with them all there.

Thanks.

- James -

01 » Now, re-write the e-mail using a formal tone. Compare it with your partner.

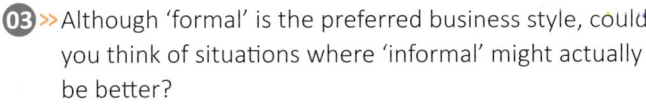

02 » Read your e-mail out loud. How does it sound compared to the informal tone?

03 » Although 'formal' is the preferred business style, could you think of situations where 'informal' might actually be better?

Brain Food

Keep in mind that formality and brevity are not necessarily opposed. The best formality might be the beauty of brevity. A longer e-mail can be counter-productive; it not only takes longer to make, but the reader might remember less as well. To achieve the best results, try to unite a formal style with a compact length.

Review   Share 3 things you learned from this lesson

💡 Sneak Peek

01 Brainstorming is important to progress and innovation; yet, some people think it is hard. Do you have any tactics to make brainstorming more successful?

02 What are some pros and cons to brainstorming in a group rather than alone?

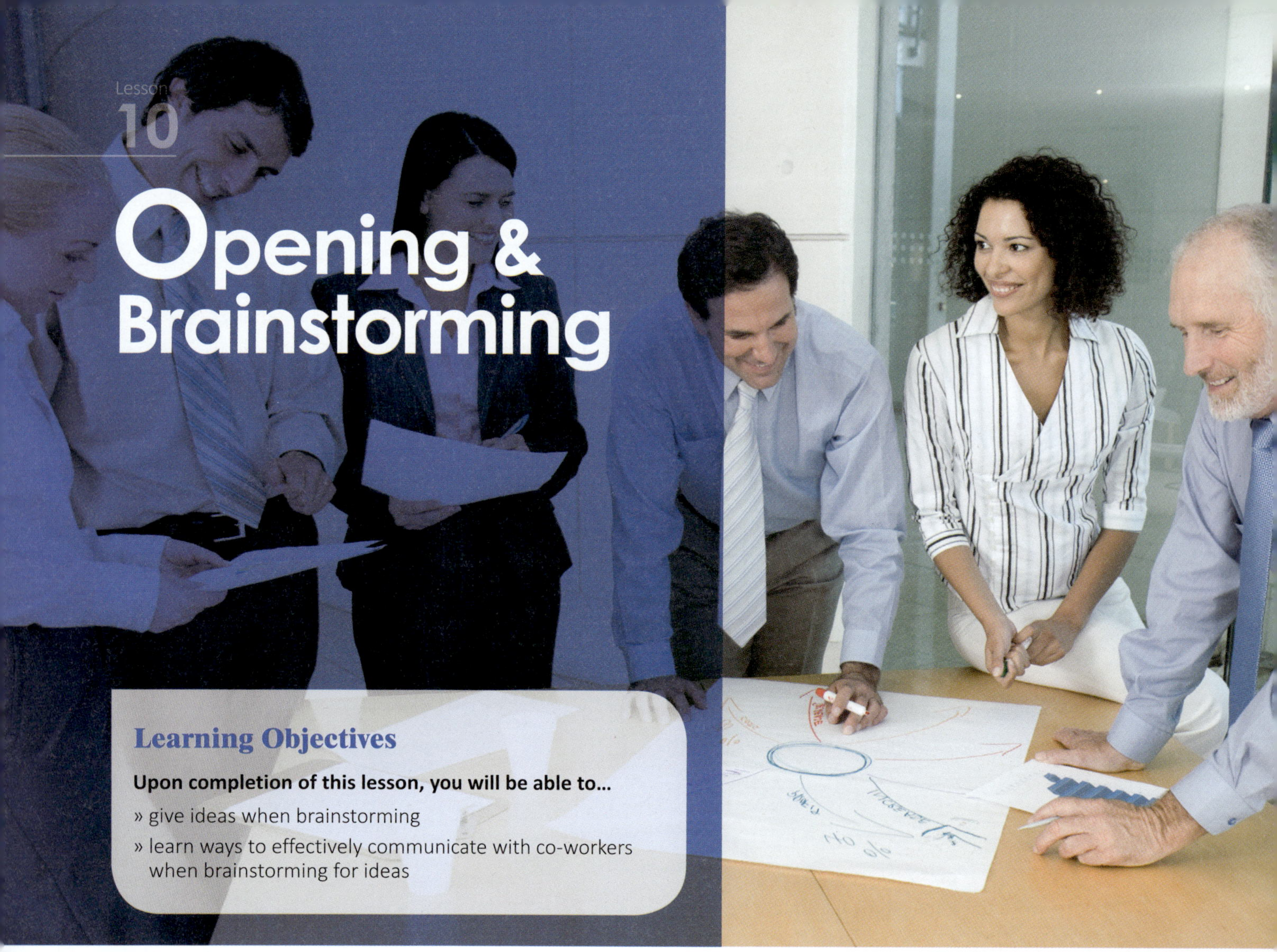

Lesson 10

Opening & Brainstorming

Learning Objectives

Upon completion of this lesson, you will be able to...

» give ideas when brainstorming
» learn ways to effectively communicate with co-workers when brainstorming for ideas

1 Getting Started

A Let's look at the image.

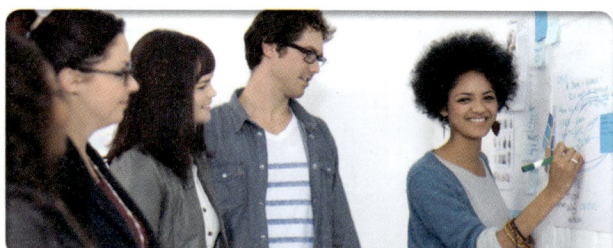

Describe the image in your own words for at least one minute.

B Discuss the following questions.

- What are some good ways to brainstorm for ideas?
- How can you catch people's attention when opening a meeting?
- Which do you think is more important? Opening of a meeting? Closing of a meeting? Why?

Good to Know
Common Mistakes

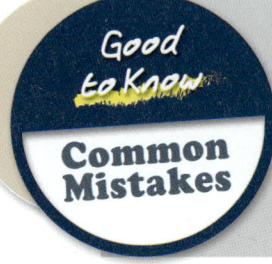

Which is right? Check the answers and explanations in the back of the book.

i.e. vs. e.g.

· I like modern abstract artists, **i.e./e.g.** Jackson Pollock, Willem de Kooning, and Mark Rothko.
· We must make a mind-map in order to see all of the possibilities, **i.e./e.g.** create a visual illustration and connect our ideas with circles and lines.
· He was famous for many qualities, **i.e./e.g.** wit and wisdom.

Lesson 10 / Opening & Brainstorming

2 Language Practice

A Business Expressions
Read the expressions and write your own sentence using the expression.

set the record straight : to make the true facts known and correct a misunderstanding.
Ex) I need to set the record straight about what happened at the last meeting.
Make your own: _____

read between the lines : to try to understand someone's true feelings about what they write or say.
Ex) Mr. James never tells exactly what he wants. You really have to read between the lines to know what he expects.
Make your own: _____

done deal : a plan that has been completed or agreed upon.
Ex) I thought the project was a done deal, but the client cancelled his order.
Make your own: _____

B Key Patterns
Here are some key patterns that you can use when brainstorming or opening meetings.

It seems that…	…better than…	Let me finish…
• we're finished • we're all here now • we need to add some more data	• A pie chart would be…a graph • I like your idea…mine • Last year's sales were…this year's	• what I was saying • organizing this data • this section at home

3 Situation & Dialogue

A Answer the following questions using the information given below.

① Look at the characters and describe the situation.
② What is the relationship between the characters?
③ What do you think will happen next?

Ms. Mable | A team member working on a project proposal.
MISSION
Show your revisions on the PowerPoint intro to Ms. Gallo, ask her what she thinks then tell her that you think you should outline the project goals first and then describe your team's plan.

Ms. Gallo | A team member working on a project proposal.
MISSION
Complement Ms. Mable's work. Agree with her ideas about organizing the presentation and offer to help edit the wording of the project goals while she takes a break.

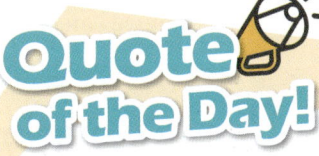

Quote of the Day!

"Imagination is more important than knowledge."
— Albert Einstein

"The best way to get a good idea is to get a lot of ideas."
— Linus Pauling

✓ Does your company require creativity? What are some ways to strengthen creativity?

✓ Do you agree with Einstein that imagination is more important than knowledge?

B Practice the dialogue with your partner.

🎧 Organizing Ideas

Ms. Mable: I just finished revising the intro for the PowerPoint. What do you think of the layout?

Ms. Gallo: The style is perfect! It's much better than the one you showed last time. It seems that we just need to talk about how to organize our ideas for the presentation.

Ms. Mable: I was thinking that we should begin by outlining our goals for the project and then describe our plan.

Ms. Gallo: You have a good plan. Why don't we type out a rough draft now? We can work out the details as we go.

Ms. Mable: That's a good idea. I'll add in the goals we discussed in the last meeting here. They're a little wordy, but we can edit them later.

Ms. Gallo: Could you put that chart on the next slide?

Ms. Mable: Okay. That looks good. I'm going to reuse some of the market statistics we found for the sales report here. How does that look?

Ms. Gallo: It's perfect. Why don't you take a break? You've already done so much. Let me finish editing the wording of the goals and then we can decide what to do next.

C Comprehension Questions

01 | What are Ms. Mable and Ms. Gallo working on now?

02 | What is Ms. Mable's plan for finishing the project? What will Ms. Gallo do next?

03 | Have you ever worked on a task with a partner or team? What are some strategies that you used to organize ideas?

4 Case Scenarios

Read the scenarios and complete each stage.

Scene 1

You are the Head of the Sales Department of Alpha Automotive Supplies. You are opening the monthly meeting. Start the meeting and invite one of the team leaders to tell about their team's progress on an ongoing project promoting a new kind of brake pad.

| **Role A** | **Role B** |
| Head of the Sales Department: Opening the meeting | Team Leader: Taking the floor to talk about the progress of a current project |

Scene 2

Your advertising firm has a new project promoting an electric car. You and a partner are brainstorming ideas for promoting it. You think the target customer would be more interested in the environmental benefits. Your partner wants to focus on the car's sleek style. Throw out your ideas and decide what to present to your supervisor.

| **Role A** | **Role B** |
| Team Member 1: Wants to focus on environmental benefits | Team Member 2: Wants to focus on car's style |

 Stage 01 Brainstorm the mission of each character.

» **Role A | Mission**

» **Role B | Mission**

 **Stage 02** How would you feel in each character's position? Explain.

Stage 03 Act out the situation. Make sure to complete the mission of each character and use the key patterns.

5 Business Basics

A Brainstorming Ideas

Brainstorming is among the most valuable skills because it can lead to the next innovation. However, it is also seen as a challenging activity as well since it can be difficult to go from nothing to something. One of the foremost strategies is the mind-map. Mind-mapping involves starting with a key idea in the middle of your page. Next, think freely to find associated ideas. Connect each new idea/term to the 'parent' idea/term from which it derives. At the end, you will have a 'web' of concepts and terms from which to work, along with a visual map of connections. Have you ever used a mind-map before?

B Share Your Thoughts

Start mind-mapping for the given issue.

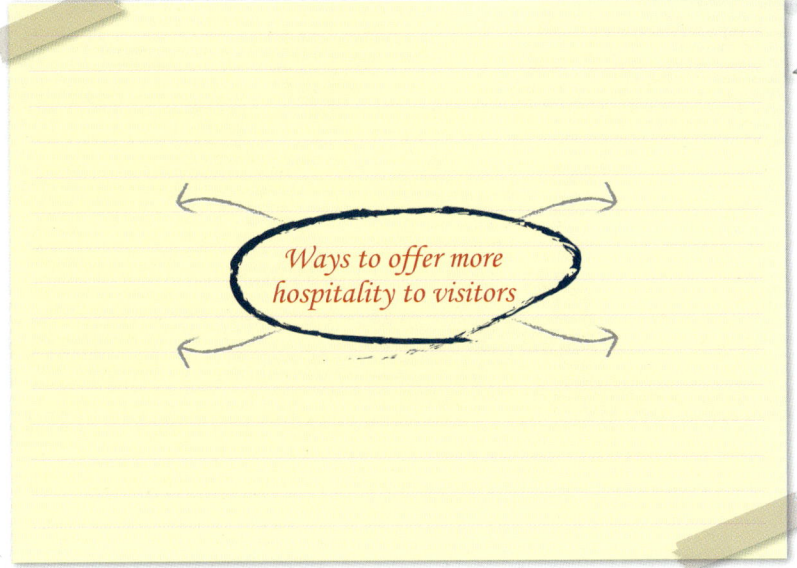

To make brainstorming easier and more productive, try to keep in mind that powerful ideas could come from relating two seemingly unrelated ideas, i.e. apparent opposites. By bringing together opposites, you can blend two things in a way that previously no one expected.

01 Share your mind-map with your partner. How is it different or similar?

02 Do you think it is better for one group to work on a mind-map together or each person individually and compare later?

03 Do you feel like you can freely express your ideas in your team meeting? Why or why not?

Review Share 3 things you learned from this lesson

💡 Sneak Peek

01 If you were traveling to another country for a business meeting, how would you get ready? Think about which steps you would take.

02 In your opinion, how many times a week is appropriate to hold meetings?

Lesson 11

Conducting Meetings

Learning Objectives

Upon completion of this lesson, you will be able to...

» preside meetings smoothly
» discuss ways to share ideas in a meeting

1 Getting Started

A Let's look at the image.

Describe the image in your own words for at least one minute.

B Discuss the following questions.

- Do you think it's better to hold meetings in the morning, during the day or at the end of the day? Why?
- What is the most effective way to maintain people's attention in a meeting (e.g. visuals, tones)?
- What is a good way to wrap up a meeting?

Good to Know — Common Mistakes

Which is right? Check the answers and explanations in the back of the book.

Between vs. Among

- The boss decided to divide the bonus equally **between/among** all the employees.
- **Between/Among** the two of you, who can do a better job?
- As the conflict **between/among** the two team members grew, an uncomfortable feeling spread between/among the team.

Lesson 11 / Conducting Meetings 55

2 Language Practice

A Business Expressions
Read the expressions and write your own sentence using the expression.

meeting minutes : notes summarizing what was said in a meeting.
Ex) *Let's begin by reading over last week's meeting minutes.*
Make your own: _____

show of hands : a vote in which people raise their hands to show support.
Ex) *Let's have a show of hands. Who is in favor of cancelling the project?*
Make your own: _____

unanimous : supported by everyone in a group.
Ex) *It appears that the feeling about the project is unanimous.*
Make your own: _____

B Key Patterns
Here are some key patterns that you can use when conducting meetings.

Whose...is it?	We'll...next time.	...is joining us today.
• data	• continue with this	• Our new manager
• turn	• formalize the plan	• A prospective client
• idea	• discuss the specifics	• A member of the sales team

3 Situation & Dialogue

A Answer the following questions using the information given below.

01 Look at the characters and describe the situation.
02 What is the relationship between the characters?
03 What do you think will happen next?

Mr. Edwards | The Head of the Sales Department
MISSION
Invite Ms. Jacobs' team to present. After the presenter presents, thank the presenter and conclude the meeting.

Ms. Jacobs | Team Leader
MISSION
Introduce Ms. Marks, the new employee in your team. Say that Ms. Marks will be presenting the team's research on expansion into the southwest.

Ms. Marks | A new member of Ms. Jacobs' team
MISSION
Greet participants and start giving presentation. Tell people that sales have grown in the last six months.

Quote of the Day!

"Let your plans be dark and impenetrable as night, and when you move, fall like a thunderbolt."
  Sun Tzu, The Art of War

"No culture can live, if it attempts to be exclusive."
  Mahatma Gandhi

✓ With which other countries, have you had meetings with?

✓ Do you think cultural differences affect businesses?

UNIT 3. Meetings & Discussions

B Practice the dialogue with your partner.

🎧 Chairing a Meeting

Mr. Edwards: Let's see. Whose turn to present is it? I think you are the last team, Ms. Jacobs.

Ms. Jacobs: Yes, that's correct, sir. First off, I would like everyone to know that a new member of our department is joining us today. I would like to introduce Ms. Marks. She started working at our company just a week ago and today, she will present about the research our team is conducting on expansion opportunities in the southwest.

Ms. Marks: Thank you for the introduction. I'm very happy to have the opportunity to share our progress with everyone. Could everyone please refer to the graph on page 2 of our report? As you can see, our sales in the region have grown considerably over the last six months.

Ms. Jacobs: We feel that the given data shows there is a lot of potential for further growth in the region.

Ms. Marks: If you look at the next page, we have outlined the strategy that we would like to follow.

Ms. Jacobs: Please look over our report. We hope to be able to share more exact data by next week's meeting.

Mr. Edwards: Thank you for your presentation. I think that's all we have for today. We'll continue with this topic next time.

C Comprehension Questions

01 | What kind of project is Ms. Jacobs' team working on?

02 | What does the team's research show?

03 | How are meetings conducted in your company? Who usually leads the meeting and how do people take turns speaking?

4 Case Scenarios

Read the scenarios and complete each stage.

Scene 1 You and your co-worker have proposed very different sales strategies during a brainstorming meeting. You want to seek out more new clients in the region while the other team member wants to make a new strategy to keep the current VIP clients. Discuss the pros and cons with each other and come up with a solution together.

Role A
Team Member 1: Wants to seek out more new clients.

Role B
Team Member 2: Wants to come up with a new strategy for VIP clients.

Scene 2 You are responsible for chairing a department meeting. All of the teams have finished their presentations. Ask the team leader to bring updated data about their current project in Greece to the next meeting. Smoothly end the meeting.

Role A
Head of the International Cooperation Department: Wants to continue the discussion next time.

Role B
Team Leader: Agrees to bring more data.

01 Stage Brainstorm the mission of each character.

» Role A | Mission

» Role B | Mission

02 Stage How would you feel in each character's position? Explain.

03 Stage Act out the situation. Make sure to complete the mission of each character and use the key patterns.

5 Business Basics

A Conducting Business Meetings

Business meetings in general can be full of tension because there might be a lot at stake. When conducting business across cultural lines, the tension could get even higher. Not only do you have to deal with the pressure of business, but you must also be sensitive to cultural rules, sensitivities, and even taboos.

	Different Meeting Cultures
U.A.E.	- Initial meetings are about relationship building more than actual business. - Meetings can seem unorganized: outside cell phone calls, text messages, and e-mails can be taken during meetings.
India	- Due to bureaucracy, decisions, approval, and processes can move slowly. You might need to hold a few meetings to achieve an agreement.
Brazil	- At an initial meeting, you might be expected to shake hands with everyone, male and female, senior and junior. - Brazilians are more lax regarding punctuality. Thus, do not get frustrated if your counterpart is not 'on time'.
Russia	- Russians can be indirect when first starting a discussion. It is considered clever; being blunt can be considered unsophisticated.

B Share Your Thoughts

01 After studying the chart above, are you able to draw any conclusions regarding those cultures?

02 Now try to find three key characteristics of your country's business culture.

Your Country	Meeting Culture
1.	
2.	
3.	

03 Why is it important to understand different countries' meeting cultures?

Brain Food

To show honor, respect, and serious intent to do business in another culture, one effective strategy might be to have your business card printed on one side in that country's language. This little step takes a bit of effort, but that extra step of effort should help you be distinguished.

Review   Share 3 things you learned from this lesson

💡 Sneak Peek

01 Have you ever offered an idea to bring big change to your company? If so, what was your idea?
02 In what kind of environment can you freely express your ideas?

Lesson 12

Sharing Ideas

Learning Objectives
Upon completion of this lesson, you will be able to...
» express different opinions
» discuss ways to positively share ideas

1 Getting Started

A Let's look at the image.

Describe the image in your own words for at least one minute.

B Discuss the following questions.

- Are you the type who strongly expresses opinions, or do you usually keep your opinions to yourself?
- What do you do when you strongly disagree with your boss? How about with your colleague?
- As a meeting facilitator, how can you create a positive environment for sharing ideas?

Good to Know — Common Mistakes

Which is right? Check the answers and explanations in the back of the book.

I vs. Me
- The representatives met with Basil and **I/me**.
- Janela and **I/me** went to the Expo together.
- Please inform Rohan and **I/me** of your decision by Monday.

Lesson 12 / Sharing Ideas

2 Language Practice

A Business Expressions
Read the expressions and write your own sentence using the expression.

get one's act together : to start to organize oneself to work more effectively.
Ex) Billy really needs to get his act together if he wants to get promoted. He's so disorganized.
Make your own: _____

stand one's ground : to hold onto one's beliefs in a disagreement.
Ex) I'm going to have to stand my ground on this issue. This is nonnegotiable.
Make your own: _____

win half the battle : to finish the most difficult part of something.
Ex) Getting the contract signed is winning half the battle. The rest of the project will be easy.
Make your own: _____

B Key Patterns
Here are some key patterns that you can use when sharing ideas.

Perhaps we should think about...	Are you saying that...?	Speaking of...
• asking for more time • how to approach the project • revising this part of the report	• we should change suppliers • the data is biased • we need to start again	• sales data, I think we need to finish our presentation • strategies, I agree with your approach • the project, let me see what you've done so far

3 Situation & Dialogue

A Answer the following questions using the information given below.
01 Look at the characters and describe the situation.
02 What is the relationship between the characters?
03 What do you think will happen next?

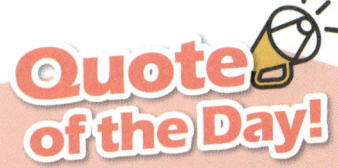

Mr. Daly | A member of the Marketing Department working on designing a new brochure for an upcoming expo

MISSION
Tell Ms. Carroll that her choice is old-fashioned and make another suggestion. Remind Ms. Carroll that you need to update the company's image.

Ms. Carroll | A member of the Marketing Department collaborating with Mr. Daly

MISSION
When Mr. Daly tells you that your choice of image for the brochure is old-fashioned, ask him what kind of image he is looking for. Then, tell him you will look for an updated image.

Quote of the Day!

"If you have learned how to disagree without being disagreeable, then you have discovered the secret of getting along."
— Bernard Meltzer

"When the final result is expected to be a compromise, it is often prudent to start from an extreme position."
— John Maynard Keynes

✓ What are some ways you can disagree without hurting the other person's feeling?

✓ Do you prefer to work with someone who always agrees, or someone who always disagrees?

B Practice the dialogue with your partner.

🎧 Stating an Opinion

Ms. Carroll:	What do you think about using this image for the new expo brochure?
Mr. Daly:	I'm not sure. It seems a little old-fashioned for our target customer.
Ms. Carroll:	What kind of image do you have in mind exactly?
Mr. Daly:	Perhaps we should think about finding something a little more modern to attract more young people. How about this one?
Ms. Carroll:	Are you saying that you want to change strategies? Target young people?
Mr. Daly:	Yes, exactly. So let's keep looking. Speaking of updating, I think we need to change some of this data in the brochure.
Ms. Carroll:	You're right. As soon as we're finished here, I'll contact Sales for some more updated numbers.
Mr. Daly:	Thanks. Here's a good one! What do you think of this picture?
Ms. Carroll:	It's perfect! You always manage to find the best pictures. Save it and I'll call about that sales data.

C Comprehension Questions

01 | What are Ms. Carroll and Mr. Daly working on? What do they disagree about?

02 | What will Mr. Daly do next?

03 | If you don't like your co-worker's idea, how do you usually approach them? What do you say?

4 Case Scenarios

Read the scenarios and complete each stage.

Scene 1
You are a member of the Sales Department. You are working with a partner to write a quarterly sales plan for your team. You and your partner disagree about some of the sales targets. You think that your partner's goal of 7% growth is unrealistic because of the current market situation. Try to convince your partner to lower the goal.

Role A | Team Member 1: Thinks your partner's goal is unrealistic
Role B | Team Member 2: Wants to raise targets by 7%

Scene 2
You are a team leader in the Marketing Department. Your subordinate has shown you his idea for a new marketing strategy for your company's line of office supplies. You feel that it is too similar to the previous strategy and fails to take into account target customers' changing needs. Your subordinate agrees, but tells you there's no time to make a new strategy.

Role A | Team Leader: Wants to hear a fresh approach
Role B | Employee: Thinks that making a whole new strategy is too time consuming

01 Stage Brainstorm the mission of each character.

» **Role A | Mission**

» **Role B | Mission**

02 Stage How would you feel in each character's position? Explain.

03 Stage Act out the situation. Make sure to complete the mission of each character and use the key patterns.

5 Business Basics

A Agree or Disagree?

In business, it's important to hear opposing ideas and challenge even the best sounding plans. However, there are two challenges regarding disagreement. First, many people seek the safety of agreement and constantly avoid any disagreement. On the other side of the spectrum, an environment of too much disagreement could lead to stalling and bickering. Disagreement is likely to be most useful when it is well-timed and well-placed through procedures to guide its application.

B Share Your Thoughts

•• **Situation**

Your company, TekTop, does much business with China by selling technology infrastructure and databases. Recently, during a visit by a Chinese leader, your co-worker Sylvia made some critical 'tweets' about Chinese leaders that were later included in a news story. Some of the Chinese business partners discovered those tweets and were displeased. As a result, when the boss found out, he decided to fire Sylvia. Sylvia, shocked, would like to protest against the decision.

01 »List reasons for agreement/disagreement with the boss's decision to fire Sylvia.

Reasons for agreement
1)
2)
3)

Reasons for disagreement
1)
2)
3)

Many CEOs refer to themselves as their company's top devil's advocate. The term "devil's advocate" refers to a person who deliberately disagrees, even and especially if their remark is not their own true opinion, as a way to open up debate and critical discussion of an issue. Having a devil's advocate can be a way to expose illogical thinking, assumptions, and other flaw and weak spots.

02 »What do think about the boss's decision?

03 »How do you think you'd feel if you were Sylvia from TekTop company?

 Review   Share 3 things you learned from this lesson

01 When you have to go on a business trip, which factors determine whether you look forward to a trip or not?

02 Do you have any 'must have' items for traveling abroad?

Business Basics 1

03 Business Problem Solving

◎ Background

Being in business means taking care of problems and surmounting challenges. Typically, the problems are related to the number one priority – making the customer satisfied. However, in business, other problems might occur due to the various inputs and factors. How you deal with problems directly relates to how you run your business. Pure Cosmetics Inc. has some internal problems that need to be solved.

◎ Tasks

01 Imagine you are one of the representatives at Pure Cosmetics Inc. Write down possible solutions and possible consequences to the listed problems below.

Problem	Possible Solution	Possible Consequence
Weak advertisement of new products	Take advantage of social platforms such as Facebook and Twitter	Might not reach out to older generation
Need people to test new cosmetics		
Late delivery problems from the suppliers		
Low quality performance of sales representatives		
Small factory size		

CASE STUDY 03

02 Now, compare your solutions/consequences with your partner. Whose solution do you think is better?

03 Next, create a table for your company or for your team. What kind of problems is your company facing? What about your team? What are some solutions? Fill out the table below.

Problem	Possible Solution	Possible Consequence

Lesson 13

Business Trip Preparations

Learning Objectives

Upon completion of this lesson, you will be able to...
» make reservations for flights and hotel bookings
» arrange meetings abroad

1 Getting Started

A Let's look at the image.

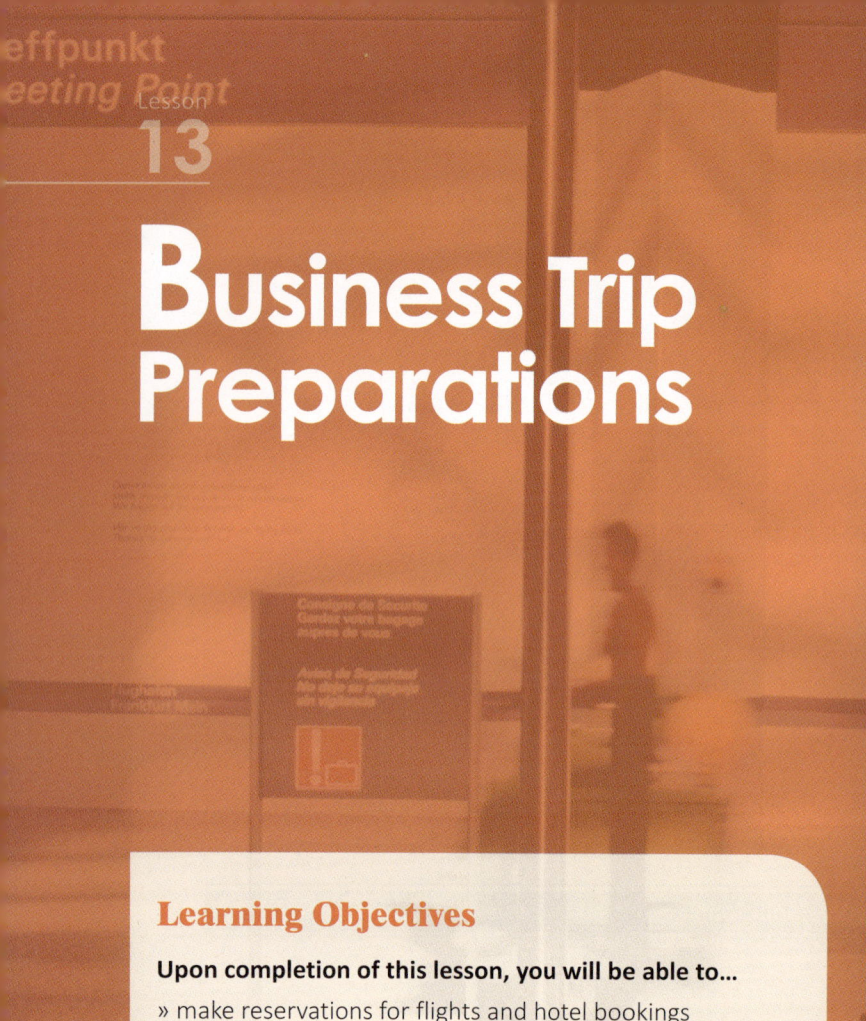

Describe the image in your own words for at least one minute.

B Discuss the following questions.

- Do you enjoy going on business trips? Why or why not?
- What is the first thing you prepare when you are assigned to a business trip?
- What is your greatest concern when traveling to another country?

Which is right? Check the answers and explanations in the back of the book.

Much vs. Many
- I don't have **much/many** books in my room.
- She doesn't have **much/many** money to buy a present.
- There's not **much/many** milk left.

2 Language Practice

A Business Expressions
Read the expressions and write your own sentence using the expression.

to the best of one's ability : as well as one can.
Ex) Alex finished the report to the best of his ability.
Make your own: _____

get the ball rolling : to do something to start an activity.
Ex) Let me get the ball rolling on this meeting.
Make your own: _____

read the fine print : to know all of the information contained in a document.
Ex) Not reading the fine print could get us in a lot of trouble later on.
Make your own: _____

B Key Patterns
Here are some key patterns that you can use when discussing business trip preparations.

I'd appreciate it if you could/would...	I'd rather...than...	I have no problem...ing
• help me with this bag	• take a taxi...the bus	• taking the next flight
• tell me where I can take the bus	• leave early...risk missing my flight	• riding the train to the airport
• confirm my hotel reservation	• fly direct...transfer	• going to the airport alone

3 Situation & Dialogue

A Answer the following questions using the information given below.

01. Look at the characters and describe the situation.
02. What is the relationship between the characters?
03. What do you think will happen next?

Mr. Davis | An executive traveling for business
MISSION
Call to confirm your hotel reservation and inquire about transportation from the airport. Ask to have a car pick you up.

Ms. McKee | A receptionist at Town Center Hotel
MISSION
Confirm Mr. Davis' reservation and give him the option of a complementary shuttle bus (leaving every 90 minutes) and private pickup for $25.

Quote of the Day!

"Everything you're sure is right can be wrong in another place."
— Barbara Kingsolver, The Poisonwood Bible

"Conflict is the beginning of consciousness."
— M Esther Harding quotes

✓ Have you met someone from a different culture and found certain cultural aspects that you couldn't understand or couldn't accept?

✓ Do you find cultural differences fun and amusing? Or do you find them irksome?

B Practice the dialogue with your partner.

🌐 Business Trip Arrangements

Ms. McKee: Hello, Town Center Hotel. Joanna speaking. How may I help you?

Mr. Davis: Hello, I'm calling to confirm my reservation for tonight.

Ms. McKee: May I have your name?

Mr. Davis: Yes. My reservation is under Lou Davis.

Ms. McKee: I found it. You reserved a Standard Room for 3 nights. Is there anything else I can help you with?

Mr. Davis: Does your hotel offer airport pickup? I have no problem taking a taxi but I would prefer to have a fixed plan for my commute.

Ms. McKee: Yes, of course. We offer a complementary shuttle bus service every 90 minutes and also private pickup can be arranged for $25.

Mr. Davis: Let me think...actually, I'd appreciate it if you could arrange private pickup for me. I have a lot of bags, so I'd rather go to the hotel directly than wait around.

Ms. McKee: No problem. Just let me know your flight details and I'll arrange it for you.

C Comprehension Questions

01 | Why did Mr. Davis call the hotel?

02 | What options did Ms. McKee give for transportation? Which did Mr. Davis choose and why?

03 | What are some things that need to be arranged for business trips? Do you prefer to make arrangements over the phone or over the internet? Explain.

4 Case Scenarios

Read the scenarios and complete each stage.

Scene 1

You were scheduled to leave for a business trip tonight, but a situation at work has forced you to delay the trip to next week. Call the airline to change the departure date of your ticket from tonight at 8 o'clock to the same time next week. The customer service representative will check the availability of the ticket for you.

Role A | Executive: Wants to change flight date

Role B | Airline Customer Service Representative: Checks availability of the ticket

Scene 2

You are scheduling a business trip to meet with a partner at Taylor, Inc. about an upcoming collaboration project. You want to visit their headquarters at the end of next week, but there is a schedule conflict. Work out another date to meet.

Role A | Project Manager at Vine Electronics: Prefers meeting at the end of the week.

Role B | Project Manager at Taylor, Inc.: Has trouble finding time to schedule a meeting

 **Stage 01** Brainstorm the mission of each character.

» **Role A | Mission**

» **Role B | Mission**

 **Stage 02** How would you feel in each character's position? Explain.

 **Stage 03** Act out the situation. Make sure to complete the mission of each character and use the key patterns.

5 Business Basics

A Culture Shock

Culture shock is also known as "transition shock" because it occurs when a person is trying to make a change between two cultures. One of the stunning aspects of culture shock is that it typically occurs after the "fascination period". At first, entering a new culture or atmosphere can seem thrilling and alluring. Later, immersion in the new culture can be full of irritants. Nonetheless, there are various ways to cope with culture shock. Let's take a look at some of the main features of culture shock.

B Share Your Thoughts

01 Look at the table below. It lists some main features of culture shock although they do not all necessarily occur. Think of a useful solution for each one.

Culture Shock Symptoms and Solution	
Symptoms	Solution
Withdrawal	
Homesickness	
Stereotyping / Hostility toward native people	
Frustration	

Have you heard of the famous phrase, "When in Rome, do as the Romans do"? It means that a visitor should adopt and adapt to the customs and manners of the people among whom s/he finds herself/himself with. Do you agree with this phrase?

02 How can companies help employees cope with culture shock? How can an individual prevent culture shock before going abroad?

03 "Reverse culture shock" occurs when a person returns to their native country but now feels out of place because they have lived in a foreign country for a long time. How do you think an individual can cope with reverse culture shock?

Review   Share 3 things you learned from this lesson

💡 Sneak Peek

01 What is your greatest concern/fear about traveling abroad?
02 Have you ever had a negative experience at an airport?

Lesson 14

Traveling Information

Learning Objectives

Upon completion of this lesson, you will be able to...
» inquire about travel information
» ask for directions and use public transportation

1 Getting Started

A Let's look at the image.

Describe the image in your own words for at least one minute.

B Discuss the following questions.

- What kind of information do you need to know before you travel anywhere?
- What should you do if you are lost abroad? How can you ask for directions?
- What are some services you can request at the hotel front desk?

Good to Know — Common Mistakes

Which is right? Check the answers and explanations in the back of the book.

Accept vs. Except

- I have tremendous news; I just **accepted/excepted** the new job offer.
- We invited suppliers, distributors, associates, **accept/except** for ex-employees.
- If you **accept/except** this delivery, that means you become responsible for its care.

Lesson 14 / Traveling Information

2 Language Practice

A Business Expressions
Read the expressions and write your own sentence using the expression.

have jet lag : to feel tiredness or confusion after a long flight.
Ex) It's been three days since I arrived, but I still have jet lag.
Make your own: ....

per diem : for each day.
Ex) We need to decide on the per diem payment for the contractors.
Make your own: ....

deadwood : people or things that are no longer useful.
Ex) We need to cut some deadwood if we want to lower our operating costs.
Make your own: ....

B Key Patterns
Here are some key patterns that you can use when confirming travel information.

Does this go (to)...?	How long will it take to get to...?	I was told that...
• the airport • City Hall • Times Square	• the conference center • my hotel • the international terminal	• the bus leaves at 1 • you called me • I need to bring my suitcase

3 Situation & Dialogue

A Answer the following questions using the information given below.

01 Look at the characters and describe the situation.
02 What is the relationship between the characters?
03 What do you think will happen next?

Ms. O'Neal | A concierge at the Palace Hotel
MISSION
Finish checking Mr. Freeman in and answer his transportation questions. Ask to see the address and find bus information for him. Give him your business card in case he has a problem.

Mr. Freeman | An executive staying at the Palace Hotel
MISSION
Check in at the hotel and ask for advice on how to get to your meeting on Park Street. Request that your luggage be brought to your room and ask if the bus is direct.

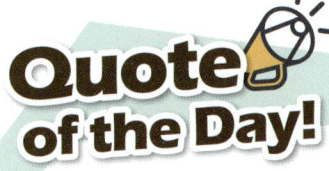

Quote of the Day!

"Travelers never think that they are the foreigners."
— Mason Cooley

"There are no foreign lands. It is the traveler only who is foreign."
— Robert Louis Stevenson

✓ Whether they mean it intentionally or unintentionally, do you think foreign travelers are generally rude?

✓ When do you feel "foreign"?

B Practice the dialogue with your partner.

🎧 Getting to the Hotel

Ms. O'Neal: Here's your key. Is there anything else I can help you with, Mr. Freeman?

Mr. Freeman: Yes. How long will it take to get to Park Street? I have a meeting there this afternoon.

Ms. O'Neal: Traffic is a little bad this time of day, so I'd recommend taking public transportation. It should take about 30 minutes. May I see the address?

Mr. Freeman: Here it is. I was told that there is a bus station nearby.

Ms. O'Neal: Yes. I think I know where this is. Let me check the bus route online.

Mr. Freeman: Could you have my luggage sent up to my room? I want to go ahead a little early to make sure I can find the building.

Ms. O'Neal: Yes, of course. Here is a map. Take the 312 bus to the Park Street stop. It leaves every 20 minutes.

Mr. Freeman: Does this go there directly?

Ms. O'Neal: Yes, it does. Here is my card. Feel free to call me if you have any problems.

C Comprehension Questions

01 | What did Mr. Freeman need help with?

02 | How will Mr. Freeman go to his meeting?

03 | What do you worry about or fear the most when going on a business trip?

4 Case Scenarios

Read the scenarios and complete each stage.

Scene 1

You are on a business trip to an unfamiliar city. You have arrived at the airport and are trying to decide how to get to your hotel in the city center from the airport. Ask an employee at the tourist information desk about the costs of various options for transportation and how long they will take.

Role A
Traveler: Needs information about public transportation and schedule

Role B
Tourist Information Desk Worker: Explains the train/bus system

Scene 2

You have arrived at your hotel. Check in at reception and ask for information about the hotel's business center. You need to print something before your meeting tomorrow and want to check what time it closes before settling into your room. The business center runs for 24 hours.

Role A
Traveler: Wants to check in and use the hotel business center

Role B
Hotel Concierge: Inform that the business center operates for 24 hours.

 **Stage 01** Brainstorm the mission of each character.

» **Role A | Mission**

» **Role B | Mission**

 **Stage 02** How would you feel in each character's position? Explain.

Stage 03 Act out the situation. Make sure to complete the mission of each character and use the key patterns.

Lesson 14 / Traveling Information   71

5 Business Basics

A Benefits of Business Travel

Business trips and traveling can be one of the most enlightening and productive experiences. If it is for the sake of business, international travel can lead to increased trade and commerce. Thus, two countries might both become wealthier through the exchange. On the downside, international travel can cause friction between different religions, races, and ethnicities.

B Share Your Thoughts

01 >> Take the following quiz and see how well you know about different cultures.

In Russia, what is the preferred way to drink vodka?	In Hong Kong, which color should you avoid wearing?	When driving in Turkey, which of the following should you be aware of?
a) Straight, no addition of anything	a) Red, it's the color of royalty so people will think you are arrogant	a) It is a Muslim country and wom-en can't drive, so men race as fast as possible.
b) Add ice to make it cooler and cut the harshness	b) White, it's the color associated with funerals and death	b) Women have the "right of way", so they typically do not yield to male drivers.
c) Mixed in cocktail drinks	c) Pink, this color is reserved for the Buddhists priests and monks	c) Smoking while driving is illegal.
d) Mixed with beer as a type of nourishment	d) Black, this color is associated with the ancient warrior class and denotes hostile attitude	d) Flashing the headlights is commonly used to indicate that the driver intends to go first or overtake.

Brain Food

When it comes to travel, it might be wise to keep in mind what Confucius said; "Wherever you go, go with all heart." Thus, whenever you travel, try to show as much interest as possible.

02 >> Review the quiz answers. How well did you do? Which question/answer surprised you the most?

03 >> Which part of your country's culture do you want to let others know about?

Answers: Russia (a) / Hong Kong (b) / Turkey (d)

Review   Share 3 things you learned from this lesson

💡 **Sneak Peek**

01 Have you ever had a negative experience at a hotel?
02 What will you do if you lose your luggage while traveling?

Lesson
15

On the Site

Learning Objectives

Upon completion of this lesson, you will be able to…
» order meals, file hotel complaints, and report stolen goods
» discuss cultural table manners and etiquettes

1 Getting Started

A Let's look at the image.

Describe the image in your own words for at least one minute.

B Discuss the following questions.

- What are some things you should check before taking foreign guests out for a dinner?
- What are some basic table manners?
- Have you ever had an unpleasant experience at a hotel? How did you handle it?

Good to Know — Common Mistakes

Which is right? Check the answers and explanations in the back of the book.

Fewer vs. Less
- You have **fewer/less** cake on your plate.
- There are **fewer/less** students in my class.
- **Less/fewer** people will come to the meeting this time.

Lesson 15 / On the Site

2 Language Practice

A Business Expressions
Read the expressions and write your own sentence using the expression.

jump to conclusions : to guess about a situation without knowing the facts.
Ex) Don't jump to conclusions about this. It's not what you think.
Make your own:

go broke : to lose all of one's money.
Ex) I'm so confident that I'm investing all my money in this company. I'm prepared to go broke on this.
Make your own:

give someone a hard time : to make things difficult for someone.
Ex) Don't take it personally. He gives everyone a hard time.
Make your own:

B Key Patterns
Here are some key patterns that you can use while working on a business trip.

I'll get back to you by...	I'd like to treat you to...	Is there any...?
• Monday • 2 o'clock • tomorrow	• a drink • coffee • lunch	• water • more bread • sugar

3 Situation & Dialogue

A Answer the following questions using the information given below.

01 Look at the characters and describe the situation.
02 What is the relationship between the characters?
03 What do you think will happen next?

Mr. Darling | A business man who has lost his briefcase during a layover

MISSION
Explain that you lost your briefcase in the executive lounge in Dallas airport.

Ms. Sane | An assistant at the Ally Airline help desk

MISSION
Offer to call the lounge to look for his briefcase. Try to give Mr. Darling a drink voucher when he has to wait for them to search for the briefcase. Get his number and offer to call him when they find his luggage.

Quote of the Day!

"When preparing to travel, lay out all your clothes and all your money. Then take half the clothes and twice the money."
— Susan Heller

"No one realizes how beautiful it is to travel until he comes home and rests his head on his old, familiar pillow."
— Lin Yutang

✓ Do you prefer to go on business trips alone or with somebody?

✓ Did you ever have to go on a long-term business trip and got homesick?

B Practice the dialogue with your partner.

🌐 Lost Goods

Ms. Sane: Hello. How may I help you?

Mr. Darling: I just arrived from Dallas and I seem to have left my briefcase in the executive lounge during my layover. Could you call and check if anyone has turned one in to the lost and found?

Ms. Sane: No problem. I'll call and check.

Mr. Darling: Thank you so much.

Ms. Sane: I'm sorry, but no one has turned one in. They are going to search and call back in an hour. I'd like to treat you to a drink while you wait. Here is a voucher that you can use at the coffee shop.

Mr. Darling: Oh that would be great. Thank you. I'll be waiting at the coffee shop then.

Ms. Sane: Then, is there any number I can call to reach you? I'll get back to you. I'm so sorry for the inconvenience.

Mr. Darling: It's no problem. Thank you for all your help.

C Comprehension Questions

01 | What is Mr. Darling's problem?

02 | What does Ms. Sane do to help Mr. Darling?

03 | Did you ever lose something important to you? What was it? How did you get it back?

4 Case Scenarios

Read the scenarios and complete each stage.

Scene 1

When you return to your hotel room after dinner, you discover that your laptop and a few other items are missing. You suspect that someone has broken into your room and has stolen them. Alert the hotel reception about the problem and ask for help to file a report with the police.

Role A
Guest: Upset about stolen goods

Role B
Hotel Employee: Apologetic about the situation and offers help

Scene 2

Your business partner has invited you out for dinner at a local restaurant. You are a vegetarian. Ask politely if there's a vegetarian restaurant and arrange a time for the dinner.

Role A
Business Partner 1: Make an invitation for a dinner at a local restaurant this week

Role B
Business Partner 2: Explain that you're a vegetarian, arrange time for the dinner

 **01 Stage** Brainstorm the mission of each character.

» **Role A | Mission**

....

» **Role B | Mission**

 **02 Stage** How would you feel in each character's position? Explain.

 **03 Stage** Act out the situation. Make sure to complete the mission of each character and use the key patterns.

Lesson 15 / On the Site 75

5 Business Basics

A Business Travel - On the Site

When traveling abroad, you are bound to encounter numerous services and attendants. How you interact with those workers will reflect strongly on your character and cultural intelligence. Even though ignorance can be permissible, having knowledge and the right manners will make you a suave and adept traveler. Therefore, it can be helpful to look at some of the differences. Let's look at the chart below.

Service/Worker	General Tipping Etiquette
Bellhop/Porter: carry your bags from the entrance to your room.	$2 per bag
Room Attendant: keeps the room well maintained to cleanliness and comfort.	$5 per day (less if less service is needed, e.g. bringing new towels only once)
Concierge: provides booking, reservations, passes, tickets, and overall insightful recommendations to make your stay full of memorable and delightful services.	$7 per day at a luxury hotel, especially for services granted

B Share Your Thoughts

01 >> Fill in the chart below and write down what you would expect to tip, be willing to tip, or think is appropriate to tip.

Service	How much would you tip?
Doorman: Holds the door open and greets you	
Sommelier: Helps you select wine	
Restaurant waiter/waitress	

Tipping is one way to recognize services rendered. It is also a way to form social relationships while still recognizing economic incentives and needs and different statuses. Nonetheless, tipping can seem puzzling and at times a hassle. However, tips are considered an implicit commitment, so it is good to make yourself aware and prepared as best as possible.

02 >> What is your experience in tipping while abroad?

03 >> How does your country's tipping etiquette compare with other countries'?

 Review Share 3 things you learned from this lesson

 Sneak Peek

01 What do you think is the most important thing to do after you come back from your business trip?
02 What are some souvenir gift ideas?

Lesson
16

Follow Up

Learning Objectives
Upon completion of this lesson, you will be able to...
» file a report on a trip
» share traveling experiences

1 Getting Started

A Let's look at the image.

Describe the image in your own words for at least one minute.

B Discuss the following questions.

- What are some first things you do once you return from a business trip?
- What are some ways to show appreciation towards the host company of your business trip?
- What are some good souvenir gifts to give to your colleagues?

Good to Know — Common Mistakes

Which is right? Check the answers and explanations in the back of the book.

Who vs. Which vs. That
- The elevator, **who/which/that** is on the left wing of the building, is under repairs.
- My boss, **who/which/that** is kind and gentle, never gets angry.
- **Who/Which/That** is a decision **who/which/that** you must live with for the rest of your life.

2 Language Practice

A Business Expressions
Read the expressions and write your own sentence using the expression.

keep someone updated : to keep someone informed on the progress of something.
Ex) I will keep you updated on our progress while you are out of the office.
Make your own: _____

have a gut feeling : to sense something instinctually without having absolute knowledge.
Ex) I have a gut feeling that this project will be a success.
Make your own: _____

make up one's mind : to make a decision.
Ex) You have to make up your mind about whom to hire. We're running out of time.
Make your own: _____

B Key Patterns
Here are some key patterns that you can use when following up on your business trip.

Is it possible to...?	I appreciate your...	Let me know if...
• send me our meeting report	• hospitality	• you need anything
• discuss the next steps	• help	• there is anything I can help you with
• call you back later	• arrangements	• you need assistance

3 Situation & Dialogue

A Answer the following questions using the information given below.

01. Look at the characters and describe the situation.
02. What is the relationship between the characters?
03. What do you think will happen next?

Ms. Barnes | A Sales Representative from Red Tech Office Equipment
MISSION
Thank Mr. Mitchell for his hospitality last week during your trip. Remind him that you will send business trip follow up report soon.

Mr. Mitchell | A Supervisor at Lily Communications
MISSION
Thank Ms. Barens for visiting. Tell her that Lilly Communications plans to continue doing business with Red Tech Office Equipment.

Quote of the Day!

"Everyone complains of his memory, and nobody complains of his judgment."
— Francois de La Rochefoucauld

"The true art of memory is the art of attention."
— Samuel Johnson

✓ What is an effective way to write a report?

✓ Discuss your most memorable business trip with your partner.

B Practice the dialogue with your partner.

🎧 Appreciation Call

Ms. Barnes: Hello, Mr. Mitchell. How are you today? Is it possible to talk now?

Mr. Mitchell: Yes. I have a little time now. I hope that you have settled in after your visit to our offices. How was your flight?

Ms. Barnes: It was a little long, but other than that, fine. I'm just calling to let you know how much I appreciate your team taking the time to show me around last week. It was really a pleasure to finally meet you all in person.

Mr. Mitchell: No, it was our pleasure. Feel free to come back and see us any time. Our company is pleased to do business with Red Tech Office Equipment and plans to keep it that way.

Ms. Barnes: We are always pleased to work with you too. Also, I will send the follow up report for my business trip by the end of this week, and please let me know if you need any assistance with our products.

Mr. Mitchell: Thank you. I will be sure to call you if we need any help.

Ms. Barnes: Well, have a nice day. I'll talk to you soon.

Mr. Mitchell: Thank you for calling. It was nice talking with you.

C Comprehension Questions

01 | Why did Ms. Barnes call Mr. Mitchell?

02 | What does Ms. Barnes want Mr. Mitchell to let her know?

03 | What are some appreciation gifts you give to the company when you go on a business trip? What are some appreciation gifts you've received?

4 Case Scenarios

Read the scenarios and complete each stage.

| Scene 1 |

Your supervisor calls you in to ask about your recent business trip. Tell your supervisor briefly that your trip was successful and that you got the customer to agree to the terms of the contract. Inform your supervisor you are still tired from jet lag and that you will need a little more time to finish your written summary of the report. Promise to hand in the report tomorrow.

Role A | Employee: Recently returned from a business trip
Role B | Supervisor: Wants to be briefed on the trip

| Scene 2 |

You have just returned from a business trip to visit a partner in India. Your boss asked you to meet with a co-worker who is making a trip to the same company next week. Tell your co-worker about your traveling experience and offer them advice on the culture.

Role A | Co-worker 1: Just returned from a business trip, give advice to co-worker
Role B | Co-worker 2: Planning for a trip next week

 **Stage 01** Brainstorm the mission of each character.

» **Role A** | Mission

» **Role B** | Mission

 **Stage 02** How would you feel in each character's position? Explain.

 **Stage 03** Act out the situation. Make sure to complete the mission of each character and use the key patterns.

Lesson 16 / Follow Up

5 Business Basics

A Writing Reports

In business, accountability is one of the highest qualities. Accountability involves tracking, measuring, and above all claiming responsibility for performance of duties. You must be able to explain what happened, why it happened, and how these results correspond to your mission. To aid thinking and discussion of business activities, business people have devised many tools such as spreadsheets and report formats.

[Look at the Information Table below. It contains the notes which Ryland made about a recent business trip to South Africa.]

Company Könstruct Equipment Ltd.
Trip Dates Monday, January 6th- Thursday, January 9th, 2014
Purpose To review and finalize sales contracts with key customers in four South African cities.

Met two business partners to discuss sales of construction machinery and building supplies.

- Ms. Kagiso Awolowo- Cape Town- Monday & Tuesday, Jan. 6&7.
  - Discussed the new highway project leading from the city center.
  - Discovered she is in the market for 2 cranes and 1 excavator.
  - Will internally discuss contract matters and confirm next week.

- Mr. Lesedi Henyekane- Durban- Wednesday & Thursday, Jan. 8 & 9.
  - Discussed the building of the 'Zoom' Finance Center.
  - Discovered that he needs 7 backhoe loaders and 3 bulldozers and 1 soil compactor.
  - Signed contract.

B Share Your Thoughts

01 Write a follow-up report using Ryland's notes. Use all the key data and organize in the proper order according to the template.

Name | Company |	Date | Nature of the Business |
· Meeting partner: · Meeting Date/location: · Meeting agenda: · Outcome: · Meeting partner: · Meeting Date/location: · Meeting agenda: · Outcome: · Follow up action to take:	

02 Now share your report with your partner. Compare your notes.

03 What do you think is the most important thing to include in a business trip follow-up report?

Brain Food

The whole idea behind business trip reporting is to create another stream of feedback and evaluation. Many streams of information and multiple levels of analysis can make a company dynamic. Shortcomings can get exposed and opportunities seized. Business trip ownership should promote ownership of the trip and its mission. Evaluation should not simply be expected but cherished by the staff as a way to keep graduating to the next level.

Review Share 3 things you learned from this lesson

Looking Back

01 Which topic in this book did you find most useful? Explain how you plan to use it in your professional career.

02 Explain some steps that you can take in order to improve or become more efficient at your job.

Business Basics 1

04 Business Hospitality

◎ Background

Often, doing business means receiving visitors and showing hospitality. Receptions at the office are typically where you would offer your guest tokens of your good will, such as a cup of hot tea or a gift bag. However, to show friendliness and amiability on a more convivial and intimate scale, many business people take their counterparts out for a tasty meal. Imagine that you will receive visits from three people each from different country. Each person has his or her own unique traits and preferences. Your goal is to match each person to the "right" restaurant for him or her.

◎ Tasks

01 Look at each person's profiles below. Get to know each character. Next, read the restaurant description. Now it is your job to take each person to one restaurant. Consider their characteristics and match each person with the appropriate restaurant.

Profile	Characteristics	Selected Restaurant
Name: Achim Wafer Company: TechPak Inc. Title: Team Leader of Sales Department Age: 33	- German - Social but conservative type - Cares about his health, likes green salads - Enjoys classical music - Loves wine	
Name: Oscar Galkina Company: Semiconductor Manufacturing Company Title: Director of Product Development Team Age: 52	- Russian - Quiet and well mannered - Tolerant of different classes and levels - Enjoys hearty meals, likes seafood and fish dish - Likes to drink cocktail	
Name: Than Ngyuen Company: Tekdesign Inc. Title: Assitant Manager Age: 28	- Vietnamese - Extremely talkative - Likes spicy foods - Doesn't drink alcohol - Doesn't like heavy meals	

CASE STUDY 04

The Fusion Garden
Food: Serves many kinds of healthy salads and dishes. Not exclusively but predominantly vegetarian. They are famous for their cocktails.

Atmosphere: Spacious with much room between tables. Restaurant is quiet and peaceful.

Cuisine de Mer
Food: High-quality French cuisine and uses the best fish from the local markets. Very famous for their good-quality wine.

Atmosphere: Very serene and tranquil, plays live music.

Classic New York
Food: Serves many kinds of sandwiches with prized meats and rare cheeses. Meals are not too heavy and can enjoy good choice of desserts as well.

Atmosphere: Good place for chatting and enjoying a meal. Can get a little boisterous but the modern fixtures put you at ease for conversation and enjoyment.

Sushi Style
Food: Serves Japanese style cuisines, multiple courses of small plates. No meat is served, but their spicy noodle special is a must-try item.

Atmosphere: Vibrant atmosphere, but more edgy than elegant.

02 Now compare your answer with your partner. Did you select the same restaurant for each person?

03 Next, write an e-mail to one of the people from the list. Invite him to dinner and give details of the restaurant.

Dear _____

I would like to invite you for a meal on ....

....

....

....

....

ANSWER KEY — Business Basics 1

Unit 1. Daily Office Routines

Lesson 1 — Welcoming Visitors

Good to Know: Common Mistakes

Everyone & Everybody
- Everyone **was** convinced that he would win the negotiation.
- I think every person in this room **is** happy.
- Everybody **has** memories of their first love.

Explanation: The indefinite pronouns "everyone" and "everybody" are always singular, although they seem to be referring to more than one person.

Lesson 2 — Organizational Structures

Good to Know: Common Mistakes

Bored vs. Boring
- The movie was so **boring**, I kept falling asleep.
- This book is so **boring**, I'm not going to read it anymore.
- The students got **bored** of studying, so they went to play outside.

Explanation: The past participle "-ed" is used to say how people feel. It refers to the receiver or person feeling the emotion. The present participle "-ing" is used to describe the people or things that cause the feelings. It refers to the actor or the thing causing the emotion.

Lesson 3 — Collaborating with Co-workers

Good to Know: Common Mistakes

Who vs. Whom
- I don't know to **whom** you are speaking.
- **Who** did you invite to the party?
- With **whom** are you discussing the new business proposal?

Explanation: "Who" is an interrogative pronoun and is used in place of the subject of a question. It can also be used in statements as the subject of a clause. "Whom" is also an interrogative pronoun, but it is used in place of the object of a question. It can also be used in statements as the object of a clause. (Who: subject, Whom: object).

Lesson 4 — Dealing with Conflicts

Good to Know: Common Mistakes

Affect vs. Effect
- The new law against smoking in restaurants went into **effect** yesterday.
- The president's speech truly **affected** me. I want to serve my country even more.
- What you do now will **affect** your future.

Explanation: "Affect" is a verb which means 'to influence'. "Effect" is a noun which means 'a result'.

ANSWER KEY 83

Unit 2. Socializing

Lesson 5 — Business Small Talk

Good to Know: Common Mistakes

Farther vs. Further
- We should discuss this topic **further**.
- **Further** input from all the groups is needed to make the best decision.
- I live **farther** outside of the city than you do.

Explanation: "Farther" is used for physical distance. "Further" is used for non-physical (immeasurable) distances.

Lesson 6 — Business Lunches

Good to Know: Common Mistakes

Then vs. Than
- Today, our team worked longer **than** yesterday.
- I will see you tomorrow **then**, right?
- Some countries are more prosperous **than** other countries.

Explanation: "Then" usually relates to time. It is most commonly used as an adverb. "Than" introduces a comparison. It is most often seen with comparatives and words like more, less, and fewer.

Lesson 7 — Formal & Informal Communication

Good to Know: Common Mistakes

There vs. Their vs. They're
- **There** were many people in the conference room.
- The analysts reviewed the data in **their** budget report.
- In the seminar room, **they're** setting up for a luncheon.

Explanation: "There" represents a place or means that something exists. "Their" is used to show possession. It is a plural possessive adjective. "They're" is a shortened version of "they are". Only use "they're" if you can substitute it with "they are".

Lesson 8 — Online Communication

Good to Know: Common Mistakes

Complement vs. Compliment
- The teamwork is great! All of you **complement** each other.
- Thank you for the **compliment**! Your praise is precious to me.
- The new software suite **complements** the existing version.

Explanation: To complement something is to enhance it or to go well with it. A compliment is an expression of praise.

ANSWER KEY — Business Basics 1

Unit 3. Meetings & Discussions

Lesson 9 — Meeting Preparations

Good to Know: Common Mistakes

Lose vs. Loose
- If you **lose** the bidding competition, then the company will have lower 4th quarter sales.
- New paint and recent improvements to the national monument already had become **loose**, so the citizens were angry.
- We need to tie up all the **loose** ends in the business expansion plan.

Explanation: "Lose" is a verb, meaning 'fail to keep, to misplace, fail to win'. "Loose" is an adjective, meaning 'not tight, not dense, or free from constraint'.

Lesson 10 — Opening & Brainstorming

Good to Know: Common Mistakes

i.e. vs. e.g.
- I like modern abstract artists, **e.g.** Jackson Pollock, Willem de Kooning, and Mark Rothko.
- We must make a mind-map in order to see all of the possibilities, **i.e.** create a visual illustration and connect our ideas with circles and lines.
- He was famous for his many qualities, **e.g.** wit and wisdom.

Explanation: "e.g." means 'for example', so you use it to introduce an example. "i.e." means 'in other words', so you use it to introduce a further clarification.

Lesson 11 — Conducting Meetings

Good to Know: Common Mistakes

Between vs. Among
- The boss decided to divide the bonus equally **among** all the employees.
- **Between** the two of you, who can do a better job?
- As the conflict between the two team members grew, an uncomfortable feeling spread **among** the team.

Explanation: "Between" applies to relational arrangements (one member to another member). Sometimes between may apply to more than two people. "Among" applies to collectives or groups (with all members involved).

Lesson 12 — Sharing Ideas

Good to Know: Common Mistakes

I vs. Me
- The representatives met with Basil and **me**.
- Janela and **I** went to the Expo together.
- Please inform Rohan and **me** of your decision by Monday.

Explanation: "I" is the subject pronoun, which means it refers to the person doing the action. "Me" is an object pronoun, which means it refers to the receiver of the action.

Unit 4. Business Trips

Lesson 13 — Business Trip Preparations

Good to Know: Common Mistakes

Much vs. Many
- I don't have **many** books in my room.
- She doesn't have **much** money to buy a present
- There's not **much** milk left.

Explanation: "Many" is used with countable nouns. "Much" is used with uncountable nouns.

Lesson 14 — Traveling Information

Good to Know: Common Mistakes

Accept vs. Except
- I have tremendous news; I just **accepted** the new job offer.
- We invited suppliers, distributors, associates, **except** for ex-employees.
- If you **accept** this delivery, that means that you become responsible for its care.

Explanation: "Accept" is a verb that means 'to receive, admit, regard as true'. "Except" is a preposition that means 'excluding'. "Except" is also a conjunction that means 'if not for the fact that' or 'other than'.

Lesson 15 — On the Site

Good to Know: Common Mistakes

Fewer vs. Less
- You have **less** cake on your plate.
- There are **fewer** students in my class.
- **Fewer** people will come to the meeting this time.

Explanation: "Fewer" is used with countable nouns including people. "Less" is used with uncountable nouns.

Lesson 16 — Follow Up

Good to Know: Common Mistakes

Who vs. Which vs. That
- The elevator, **which** is on the left wing of the building, is under repairs.
- My boss, **who** is kind and gentle, never gets angry.
- **That** is a decision **which** you must live with for the rest of your life.

Explanation: "Who" refers to people. "That" or "which" refers to groups or things. "That" is used to introduce an essential clause while "which" introduces nonessential clauses. When any of the words "that, this, these, those" have already introduced an essential clause, "which" can be used to introduce the next clause regardless of whether it is essential or nonessential.